Marcell Garretson is ‹ ~~years I have watched r... j... ...j ... ...~~ *inspiration to anyone who meets him. Knowing him today, you could never believe he is the same person you will read about in this book. I found his story to be magnetic; once I picked it up, I couldn't put it down. This testimony of Marcell Garretson is a must for everyone to read.*

Rich Scherber,
Minnesota Teen Challenge Executive Director

Reading Marcell Garretson's account of abuse and crime in his life, you may wonder, "Is there any hope for the community?" Then as chapter six ends there is a glimmer of light, but will it go out? Read his account of the Holy Spirit's work as the transformation to faith and obedience transpires. A person who was "helpless to protect the people [he] loved" is dramatically changed. Love is both submitting to the will of God and a gift from God. Each person's story is different. God has called Marcell to reach out to those released from prison that they too might start a new life.

Al Quie, Former Governor of Minnesota

Conviction
by Marcell Garretson with J.K.Olson

Cover sketch by Cathy Dewitt
Cover design by Sally LaPorte and Cathy Dewitt

CONVICTION

*By Marcell Garretson
with J.K.Olson*

*Dedicated to my mother
for her unconditional love and support
throughout the years.*

*A special thanks to
my Lord and Savior Jesus Christ,
my wife for her tender support and patience,
my children for their understanding,
my church family for all of their prayers,
and to Jill Olson for sitting down with me
and bringing out my story.*

-1-
My Heritage

When I started school in the 1960s, I was called Yellow Boy. It didn't mean much to me that my father was black and my mother was white, until I was surrounded by other kids. That's when I first realized there wasn't a place for me. Most of the kids in my class looked like my mother, a few looked like my father, but I didn't look like either.

I didn't know my grandparents, or any of the relatives that flow down from them—aunties, uncles, and cousins—so I looked only to my parents to tell me who I was. My dad was African American. He was tall, dark, and handsome, and carried a .44 Magnum inside his denim overalls. His name was Louis Thomas, but people called him Big Lu; he was a pimp, with a reputation for violence. One of my earliest memories is of my father pistol-whipping my mother. When I was five or six, he cracked her in the head with a chair. The chair broke in pieces; she fell to the floor and didn't move for a long time.

I knew little about where my dad came from, or his family. My kin. I knew he was raised in Monroe, Louisiana, born early enough to hear stories from old-timers, leaning on their canes, of life before the Civil War. My father was a few generations away from the war, but it was likely handed down to him in the words of eyewitnesses. He probably heard from the generations who came along after the war, when irrational mobs decided who lived and who died and law enforcement sat idle. That was still happening when he was coming up; He was in his forties when I was born in 1959. It's possible that anger built up in his heart and then came blasting out years later, pressed hard and sharp over time like a diamond.

Besides a love of biscuits and gravy, which he ate for breakfast, that anger was the only thing he brought with him from the South. It also drove him from it. As an adult, I heard that my father had left Louisiana and changed his name after he killed a white man. But like any story that has existed over the years by

1

word of mouth, any change in the wind could have rearranged the facts. His violent temper was also likely fed by extreme poverty. The only story he told of his childhood was of him sitting on the kitchen floor and biting his mother in the leg because he was hungry. By the time he passed the story to me, he told it laughing.

It could be that his violence also came from the roots of our family tree, passed to him in a genetic package, like a high IQ or a space between your teeth. But since I never climbed or set eyes on my family tree as a child, I can't say for sure. We were about as far north as you could get from Louisiana in this country, and it didn't survive the winters, I guess.

When he left his family and the South, my father didn't let his seat in the black section of a bus or a train keep him from going places. I don't know how he traveled, but I know he moved around the country like it was a Monopoly board, looking for opportunity. He used to brag about how he'd been from the rocky coast of Maine to the Golden Gate Bridge. He probably poured his charm on and pulled his chair up to as many gambling tables as would take his money.

By the time he put roots down in Minneapolis, known as a place for prospects, he had spent his youth and was ready to build a future, a money-making kingdom. He probably worked his wiles and handed out promises to women like he was running for office. He may have targeted white women because of their reputation for being gullible. When I was growing up, I noticed a lot of black men/white women relationships, and nearly all of them were abusive. When my dad was growing up in the South, black men could not even give a white woman eye contact. A lot of the abuse that black men showed white women was revenge for the degradation they had been through, I believe.

One white woman, desperate for hope, heard my father's smooth lines and ended up swallowing the hook. My mother connected with big-talking Lu, sixteen years her senior, and stepped through a door that would slam behind her forever. Geraldine Garretson, a small-town white girl from Wisconsin, became pregnant with me while walking the streets for my dad. Back then, race mixing (often referred to as just "mixin'") was looked on as the devil's work by many. Her family would have nothing to do with her after she had me.

When I started school, I had to choose a color. Since trying to be friends with both would mean rejection by both, I chose to belong with the ones who walked my neighborhood and looked the most like my father. I felt bad and even angry when they'd bad-mouth or beat up on a white kid, but I kept it inside.

In the 1960s, everybody in my neighborhood wanted to be a pimp. Only the preachers and the pimps tooled the neighborhood in big cars, their diamond-studded fingers angling out the window. The pimps were tough, and my dad was no exception.

He wore wingtip shoes and a derby hat, bent up on one side over his ear. His shirts were bright-colored silk under overalls pressed smooth as a piece of ice. His hair reached down his back, and women would style it for him with a hot comb and hot curler. His goatee was gray and trimmed close.

Besides him raising a hand to my mom, I don't have much for memories of my father at home, except once when he robbed a liquor store and came running in the house for a place to hide. (When the police came to the door, I piped up, "You come looking for my dad? He's in the back room!" That is the only early memory I have of him. Hard to forget, since both my mom and dad teased me about it for years.)

My father was also a bootlegger. He sold liquor from the trunk of his car, and every night people would come by our house to keep partying after the bars would close. Our living room was filled with people, lying around the room in varying degrees of intoxication. From sober (my mother), to loud and obnoxious, to passed out cold. I would go through the house and sneak drinks from hundreds of bottles.

Occasionally my father would bring me to the bars with him. The old women at the bar, mostly former prostitutes, would gush about how cute I was and give me money. So I would make the rounds and my father would regularly collect the money to buy more drinks. I didn't mind: he took me places and called me his son; he let me ride shotgun before I could see above the dashboard;

he called me Junebug. I would learn later that I looked like his brother, a man I never met, who was nicknamed Junebug.

"Dad, some day I'm gonna buy you a Cadillac," I'd say. He didn't make fun of that young ambition. Sometimes people would point me out and say, "That's Big Lu's son." Now and then folks called me "Little Lu." I lived on those words for a long, long time.

My father said to me, "I wouldn't take fifty million dollars for your baby toe." He didn't show that side of his personality to many. He had battle scars from those who could fight back against the rage that so often ruled him. Two fingers on his left hand were forever bent because he had been stabbed in the wrist. He walked with a limp after someone shattered his kneecap with a bullet. I remember visiting him in the hospital after that, wishing I could kill the guy who did it. I guess I was five or six years old.

But my mother saw the inside of a hospital the most. "Your father always loved guns," she said to me. "Once he told me, 'I'm gonna kill you!' and he hit me with his gun. A friend helped me to the hospital. It's not like I was innocent…but I got so tired of the abuse, I just left."

My dad wasn't at home enough for me to know when he was gone. After they split, I spent time with my father in his apartment, where he would feed me alcohol. I drank it because I wanted to please him, and because it made me tough and bold. Everybody drank; it was the lifestyle. At his house, there were often women, white and black, walking around without clothes. My father would point one out and invite me to "go get her." That was also part of the lifestyle. Some of those "wild oats" that he sowed took root. I had a half sister who lived in the projects at the same time I did. She was a few years younger than me; I just knew who she was and that her name was Lisa. It was a little awkward when I saw her. I also heard of another sibling I had never seen named Thomas.

My mother says she didn't work the streets much after she had me, but it was enough for me to remember seeing her walk through the house with strangers. They'd go to the bedroom in the back and shut the door. I hated those men.

4

When I was five, my mother became pregnant with a trick baby. My father signed my brother Gerald's birth certificate and treated him like a son, even though it was obvious he wasn't. My brother's skin matched the color of the snow that fell the January he was born.

From the very beginning, Gerald was mine. He followed me around and called me Gungung—his toddler version of Junebug. But he stood out in our neighborhood like the moon in the night sky. And, much as I wanted to be feared like my father was, it would soon become apparent that I couldn't protect the ones who needed me the most.

-2-
Criminal Beginnings

Even as a child, I'd always known it was my job to emotionally support and protect my mother. She depended on me because she had no one else. That was a pattern in her life that started a long time before I came along.

When my mother was five years old, her mother died in childbirth. Her father then gave my mom to her aunt and uncle in Minneapolis. (He kept his other three children, all sons.) She said those early years in her new home were the best in her life. Later, her uncle started sexually abusing her, and by the time my mom was a teenager, she had become a "problem child," as it was defined in the early 1950s: smoking cigarettes, skipping school, and running away. When she wasn't in a juvenile detention center, she was hanging with a wild crowd on Lake Street, avoiding school altogether. After seventh grade, she never went back, and no one tried to change that.

My mother married a military man when she was 17. They settled near his family in West Virginia, and she had three little boys by the time she was 22. One morning, after learning of her husband's unfaithfulness, she woke early and went to the back porch. When her oldest wandered from bed and went to her side, she sent him back in to his bed. She came into the house later and found it filled with smoke. She was able to get to the youngest two and take them out as the house burned, but she could not find her oldest, her four-year-old, in time. His body was later found behind the kitchen door. Fifty years after, she doesn't talk about the memory without tears and her hand coming up over her face.

At the time, she dealt with it by running away, leaving her children with her mother-in-law. She ran back to Minneapolis where she met my father, who I'm quite sure sold her a bill of goods. They probably wouldn't have married, even if it would have been acceptable. But he "turned her out," with his characteristic persuasion, I'm sure.

She constantly talked about her boys, crying, when I was coming up. But she knew, once she had me, there was no turning back. She lost the inheritance she would have had from her aunt and uncle; they didn't speak to her again after she had me. It was 1959, and she was a white woman with a black baby and no one to fall back on. It wasn't long before the protection she felt with my father came at too high a cost, and she left.

I would still spend time with my dad. Once, when I went with him to buy liquor, someone was playing with a gun and it went off. The bullet passed between my father and me and went into a refrigerator behind us. That type of thing was not uncommon in my neighborhood, where everyone carried. Those were the days before permits; everyone had a gun with them while partying with drugs and alcohol and the opposite sex. It was all part of the lifestyle, and it all happened at my dad's place.

When he married my stepmother, a black woman everyone called Big Momma, she would sell a dish of Polish sausage in a bun with chili on top during the after-hours parties at their house. Every bootlegging house sold some kind of snack during party hours, which was nearly every night.

Although my mom didn't drink much or do drugs when I was growing up, she partied with people who did. There were a lot of one-night stands, lots of guys coming and going. We kids would just go where everyone was gathered for the night. Sometimes my mom would leave us with friends and be gone for days—with men, or because she was arrested on prostitution charges.

Eventually, Gerald and I ended up in foster care. He was about three years old when we were placed in a home with two girls my age or older. Because he was white and small for his age, Gerald was often targeted in our neighborhood. He also showed off, trying to prove he belonged, which resulted in a lot of fighting. I felt like I had to be by his side at every minute to protect him. In this foster home, the girls started fighting with Gerald and one pushed him into a radiator, splitting his head open. As he left for the emergency room, a fear burrowed deep into me: I was failing in my job as protector. At eight years old, I was helpless to protect the people I loved.

Gerald considered my friends his friends and tried hard to fit in with the older kids everywhere he went. When we were adults, he told me he thought of himself as mixed race, just like me. So when kids sneered "little white boy" at him on the street, he took it like a slap in the face and came at them fists first. I also defended both of us against bullies.

There were days when the bell rang at the end of the day, and I just hit the sidewalk running. I always had to be looking over my shoulder. There were some kids in our neighborhood who were a few years older than me and they had it in for us. Once, after they worked me over pretty good, my dad said, "What happened to you?" He was *mad* when I told him. We got in the car and, without saying a word, he took me down to a place where a gang met. I was part of that gang as soon as I walked through the door with my dad, simple as that. I don't remember their names or any details about them, but I know they didn't argue with my dad. No one disagreed with Big Lu, "The Godfather," as he was sometimes called. This gang was all late teens or early twenties; I might have been 13. This was my father trying to make me tough, because being tough meant not only survival, but success. He also had a reputation to maintain; he didn't want a son who was a wimp. That was the relationship we had. It would have been different if we could have talked about things, and he didn't judge me. But he just left me there.

I sat silently, listening to them make plans to spring a friend out of a state prison. *State* prison! Then we got in the car and headed to Cozy's Bar. I sat in the car, and when they were all inside, I ran home. I may not have been as tough as I wanted to be, but I was no fool. I wasn't about to be part of a state prison break.

That was the extent of my gang involvement. The gang I hung with were friends, mostly my mother's friends' kids, younger than me, and mixed race. My mother's friends were white women dating or married to black men. There weren't many then, and they stuck together. They were the ones who took her to the hospital after my father beat her.

Barb was one of my mother's good friends. Since Gerald and I didn't have the family that other kids had—no grandparents or aunties or cousins of our own to spend the night with, or get attention from on our birthdays—and since Barb's kids were cut off from their relatives too, we started calling each other cousins. Barb said that there was nothing we didn't know about each other.

We'd stay out all night, me and Gerald with her boys Rob and Little Man, looking for "opportunity." It came one night at the back door of a warehouse. We kicked in the panel of a garage door and started relieving that building of as much loot as we could, mostly cigarettes, candy and pop. We went back every night for two weeks, loading up wagons and maybe a grocery cart, then bringing it back to the basement of the projects. Then, from our card-table shop set up on the sidewalk, we sold mostly to older welfare ladies from the projects. With money in our hands and a seemingly endless supply, we were in hog heaven for about two weeks. Then they nailed the panel back in place. That was my first taste of business and I was hooked.

Since most of our gang was younger than me, I organized other ways to make money and they followed along. I would send them down to Broadway Avenue to snatch purses. When they came back, I would divide up the goods between all of us. Sometimes I would go with them; sometimes I would go by myself. I hoped the whole while that I didn't hurt anyone. I would often target older ladies, who gave up easier. But if they hung on, and started hollering in the street, I ran. Broadway was all white then, unlike today.

We didn't break the law for profit only. When me, Gerald and Rob found an old, push-button car down by the railroad yard on Glenwood with a six-pack of Grain Belt beer in the front seat, that was invitation enough. The police caught us about four miles and six bottles later. Gerald and Rob got away through a hole in the floorboard in back. I was taken to the juvenile center and released after a few hours.

Crime and its fallout was something we saw daily. One night when we were walking near 13th and Knox, we came up to a white guy slumped over the steering wheel of his car. He didn't look like he belonged in our neighborhood. Once I got closer, I saw he didn't have much chance of leaving. The others were too afraid, but I walked up to the window and shook him by the shoulder. He fell back, and I could see two things: he had been shot in the head, and the passenger seat was covered with coins. I reached in, moved his arm out of the way, and grabbed a handful of that change.

Another time, older kids traveled in a pack down Plymouth, smashing their way into businesses, swinging for whatever they could destroy or take down. I used my crowbar to get into the washers of a laundromat that had been destroyed. It wasn't until looking back at it years later that I realized the chaos was caused by the assassination of Martin Luther King Jr. I knew somebody important had died, but I was too busy to care. One of the darkest hours for African Americans in this country was a day I spent happily filling my pockets with someone else's laundry money.

The Bible says to train up a child in the way he should go, and when he is old he won't depart from it. That was true in my case: I was trained to become a criminal, and I started swinging for the fence as early as I could, with no remorse.

We lived at the Fourth Avenue projects, near Olson Memorial, when I learned about sniffing household products—or huffing, as it's called now—from the Native Americans. The projects were advanced in one respect: there was no segregation. We all lived together; we all sinned together; we all took our loneliness, insecurities and inadequacies and buried them in the drugs that were within reach of our young hands at the time. That high would take us to a place where everything was better. At seven or eight years old, I couldn't recognize what all the problems were, but I knew I preferred the world that huffing brought me to. I was laying down tracks that I would follow well into my adult life. Escape was an easy route to take; substance abuse was on every block in my neighborhood.

Like all kids in the late '60s and '70s, we tooled around on our bikes. Those two wheels gave us the neighborhood. For us, a bike was either a gift—left to us by someone who had walked into a store and left it up against a wall or a tree—or it was pieced together from parts I found in the alleys. A bike was a status symbol, and after I taught Gerald to ride, I made sure we both had nice ones.

Gerald was my passenger the day he was old enough to hang on. He usually rode up front. I'm sure we looked odd, especially in the '60s: a black boy cruising around town on his banana seat bike with a little white boy sitting up front on those sissy handlebars. Sometimes we would bike out to Theodore Wirth Lake. Gerald would climb onto my back and I would swim us out to the raft. I would make him swim back on his own. That toughened him up, I thought. He later said it taught him how to swim. We would also bike down to Lake Calhoun during Aquatennial, a summer celebration held every July. People made boats out of milk cartons for a race and would leave them tied up at the dock before the race. Gerald and I took those boats out for a ride every year when we were younger. We sank a couple every summer.

After my dad was out of the picture, my mother went through a string of other men. One was Matthew. I remember Matthew's black, shiny bald head, and that he worked in a shoeshine shop downtown. He gave us Rock 'Em Sock 'Em Robots for Christmas. He seemed like a decent guy, but that lasted about four or five months, I guess, and then he was gone.

Then she started seeing someone she met through Barb. Curtis was an ex-military man, with a steady job. I think by this time, my mom was desperate for security.

Her only income was welfare or men. She'd been through many different relationships since my father, so maybe marriage seemed a relief.

Curtis lived with us for a short time before they were married, and things seemed okay. He managed to control himself during their live-in period. But once they were married, and we had moved from the projects into a house on Oliver, he felt free to start expressing himself physically.

Shortly after they were married, I remember running with my mother and Gerald and baby sister to Rose's house across the street. I shoved the icebox against the door to keep Curtis out. He slammed his body against the door again and again while my mother cried uncontrollably and all us kids leaned hard to keep him out until the police came. With the help of terror-induced adrenaline, we did it. After Curtis was released the next day, things went right back to the way they were.

The next twenty years of my mother's life would hold almost constant abuse. He swore at her daily, his anger sparked by the smallest things: a late meal, something someone said or did during his day that would fester and explode in her face when he got home. The only thing predictable about our life was its unpredictability. He was an alcoholic, and his rare moments of decency were always tempered by alcohol. It wasn't always safe when he was drinking, but it was often enough for us to hope he was drunk when he was home.

When he would get angry, he'd start arguing with my mother, slapping her face, sometimes slapping her off her chair. Eventually, he'd come after me. He often hollered about my dad during his fits. He hated my father. I think seeing my face brought that hatred front and center. He used his fists on me.

But I think what hurt the most was his words. I kind of looked up to him, like I did my father. But his razor sharp tongue cut me down again and again. His two-part proclamation was regular: "You're stupid!" and "You'll never amount to anything." And occasionally, "You're worthless like your dad!" It crushed something deep inside me.

I'm sure my mother felt helpless to stop it. When my mother and I were out together, "White trash!" would sometimes come at her from both black and white, and I would see her cry. She didn't wear a mask. She carried burdens that wrapped around her soul like barbed wire, but she never let that sadness or abuse harden her. She was kind and giving to others, letting kids stay at our home when they needed a place. I tried to take care of my mother and protect her as best I could, and she looked to me for guidance and protection like I was an adult. I hurt for her when Curtis and other people would hurt and insult her, but I didn't let that show.

Curtis was six feet tall and earned every dollar of that steady paycheck working with his back at the foundry. When he was violent, there was nothing I could do to stop him except stand and be the decoy, drawing him away from my mother and brother. Eventually, Curtis started threatening to kill me. When things became more than I could stand, I took Gerald and went to the streets. We would go downtown to the Radisson or the Drake and creep into the stairwells. Hotels didn't lock their outside doors then, so we would bed down in the stairwell until someone found us and kicked us out. But mostly, whether we ate or not depended on whether we were successful in crime. Whether it was tips off tables at Big Boy, or lunches from the break room of the railroad depot off Seventh and Olson Memorial, stealing wasn't a game then.

Sometimes Gerald and I would go into Dayton's and Donaldson's department stores on Nicolet Avenue, grab fur coats or fringed vests, and run out and over to Hennepin Avenue for a quick sale with the pimps and hustlers. It was then that I started to fantasize about that lifestyle. The contacts that I made then would become my fences later, when it became a reality for me.

Gerald and I would last a couple of weeks on the street before getting caught. By then we were ready for a hot meal and a bunk. We told them at the juvenile center that we wanted to stay. But they told us, "You gotta go home." They didn't want to house and feed petty thieves.

It wouldn't be long before we were earning our keep.

3

I Learn I'm 'Special'

I started school ten years after segregation was outlawed. Occasionally I would act up in class—either clowning or fighting—and get the broad end of a paddle on my hand or the back of my arm. Times have changed.

In my neighborhood, school officials pushed the black students through the system. I was never held back, even though I couldn't read. I had some private tutoring when I was in grade school, which I endured. But I didn't learn to read until later, when I was in prison.

In grade school, I skipped as often as I could, which brought Mr. James, the truancy officer, to my mother's door. I was happy that he made house calls because by then I was ashamed that my mother was white. My mom told me later that when Mr. James came by, he would hit on her. I don't think there was an exchange of services. But it didn't seem to be a problem getting back into school.

When I got to junior high, the tutoring stopped and they classified me as Special Ed so I would graduate. That was okay with me. I considered myself a student of the street more than anything. They didn't have the same labels they have now, but I'm quite certain all of us "Special Ed" kids were attention deficit. This was a class of disadvantaged kids, mostly African American males: physically or mentally disabled kids with coping problems and anger issues. That was a time, the early '70s, when a lot of families were coming up from the rural South—Mississippi, Alabama, Georgia. Many were poor, uneducated farm kids. I remember those kids not by their names, but by what we called them. And I remember seeing a lot of them die early in life. One classmate we called Country was killed on Broadway Avenue in Minneapolis when he was 18. He was arguing with a bouncer at a bar when the guy pulled a gun and shot him. Another kid we called Dirtbomb, from Oklahoma, was hit by a truck and killed when he was 16.

During one year of junior high I went to Lincoln Learning Center, an alternative school for troubled kids. They paid us $8 a day at that school just to show up. I made a desk for my dad in a woodworking class. I also made more contacts with budding criminals. After one year at the alternative school, I was back at Lincoln Junior High School as a Special Ed student again.

Though I still tried to stay away from school as much as I could in junior high and high school, I made friends that I would keep throughout my life, committing crimes alongside them. As young teens we would go up to Lowry Avenue, into the white neighborhood, and knock on a front door. If no one came, we'd either walk in, since often the doors were left open, or we'd get in through a window. Some of my friends had their heads blown off doing this. But that didn't stop me. The drive for what the money could buy—drugs, alcohol, and clothes or stuff to make me look cool—was greater than my fear of what could happen if I was caught. Besides, I never thought I would get caught. I was a student of the street, and one of the best, I thought.

The Mack and Superfly movies in the '70s were an altar call for all young men in my neighborhood. We dedicated our lives to the glamorous and powerful lifestyle of the hustlers and pimps. The fancy cars, the jewelry, and the women all belonged to the ones who rose to the top. A goal was confirmed as we watched those movies. No one doubted that my classmates and I were headed for life on the street, and they were right. If we could have known how that lifestyle ends, I'm not sure we would have changed our course. The deception was so real. And the alternatives so few. I had to get a little farther down the road to see the truth—that the pimps and hustlers don't live a long life in a new loft downtown, surrounded by their wealth and women. There weren't any retiring to the suburbs to give the grandkids rides on their John Deere lawnmowers. One classmate of mine from Lincoln Learning Center is doing life for killing a police officer. Some of my old friends are now locked up in the psych ward. And some are dead. We all started out wanting to rule the streets.

Gerald was different from me in that he was smart. But he was looking up to the same people on the same streets that I was, and he didn't have much hope, or desire, to be different. He still seemed to be targeted. One day we were at our cousin's house when his father came home and accused us of stealing from him and—someone had actually done this—taking a dump on his bed. We tried to tell him we didn't do it, but it was too late. He went into the bathroom without a word and started the water running in the tub. We knew he was crazy, but we never expected what he did next. He came back into the room, grabbed seven-year-old Gerald and carried him into the bathroom. He shoved his head under the water and held it down. I hollered at the guy, and both Little Man and I were beating on his back. I was terrified. When he decided to let Gerald go, he turned and beat on us until we ran out.

Gerald had gotten into trouble and been to juvenile detention centers a couple times when my mother's brother Ross and his wife asked if he could live with them. Ross had come back into my mother's life as an adult, and now he and his wife were living in Apple Valley, a suburb south of Minneapolis, with no children of their own. I'd seen the suburbs from a bus window and I knew the city was raggedy by comparison. Although Gerald had visited, my mom and I had never been out to see Ross's house. But I knew if it got him away, it would be better for him.

I've always said that I was 12 when they took him from me. It was like losing a part of me—or, even though I wasn't yet a teen, like losing my own child. In the dark, with the top bunk over me empty, I couldn't stop my grief from coming out in tears. I would never have admitted that to anyone. I was a teenager then, and was struggling even more with feeling awkward—trying so hard to fit in and look good.

I was now using acid and PCP, committing more burglaries and robberies, still mostly purse snatching. Also, at 13, I moved my girlfriend into my bedroom. This was okay by my mother and Curtis because they thought it would keep me home more, off the streets.

Gerald would come home occasionally, wearing new clothes, Converse shoes, and have money in his pocket. But he was more interested in hearing than telling. He wanted to find out about what was happening in the neighborhood.

After one year, without any trouble with the law, Clifford asked Gerald if he wanted to live with them forever. "You don't want to go back to those dogs," they told Gerald. (He didn't tell me they said this until we were adults.) The line had been drawn in the sand, and for Gerald, there was no question about which side he belonged on. Right after that, he stole several silver dollars from them, was caught, and sent him back home to us.

I was happy to have my brother back. But when he was gone, I had become a teen and was now used to having my friends to myself. For the first time, he started making his own friends, and it didn't take him long to continue his life of crime with other partners, or alone.

Gerald has always had a love of luxury cars, especially Cadillacs. When he was eight he decided he'd gone long enough without one. Don't ask me how he saw over the dashboard when he drove off. From then on, he was in and out of institutions so much, he wasn't home for Christmas again until he was 40 years old.

After one release from juvie, Gerald came home with an afro. I would wear a pick in the back of my afro with the Black Power symbol of the raised fist. He tried the pick in his hair, but it wouldn't hold it; his hair was too soft. He kept that hair for a decade anyway.

Our stepfather Curtis was our male role model, or influence, for many years. And *his* main influence was alcohol. When Curtis *didn't* drink, he would sit by himself in the bedroom. And he was mean. When he *did* drink, he would sit out in the living room. And he was mean. We kids used to hope and pray that he was drunk when he was home, because his occasional decentness was always influenced by alcohol. Yet there were times, which no one could predict, when he went beyond mean.

I came home one day to find him filled with alcohol and rage. His hatred had my name on it, and at one point he ran to pull out his gun. When I realized what he was doing, I ran in terror. He caught me on the basement steps and held the barrel of that shotgun to my temple.

"You want to be a worthless pimp like your father, don't you?" he yelled. I knew he had it in him to pull that trigger. He wanted to do it, I thought. I saw the end of my life there on the stairs. I remember thinking that I really hadn't lived yet.

My mother was screaming at him to stop, and eventually he stumbled back up the steps with the gun. I ran to my father's house, leaving the sounds of my mother's cries behind.

I lived with my dad until I was picked up on theft and truancy charges a year later and sentenced to Hennepin County Home School. Six months later, I escaped and went back home to dad. It wasn't hard to get away back then because the place wasn't locked up. Kids walked off all the time. I just strolled up the railroad tracks and came home.

When I got there, my stepsister told me that my dad had gone down south to see his family. I was bummed for missing out on going. He had never gone home before. Looking back, I realize that was a sign that the end was near. I think he was looking for closure.

Shortly after he came home, I stole a gun from my mom's neighbor. My dad proudly took me down to the hustlers on Plymouth to sell it. We were both surprised when the first person we showed it to said to me, "Boy, that's my gun." I denied it, but we followed him back to his house—the house I'd been in just minutes earlier—so he could check under his bed for the gun. Nothing but dust. This is where my father started talking. His words were as smooth as liquor, taking away all sense of consequence and reality. The man didn't press charges.

A few months later, I was again doing time at the home school when I received a call from my mother. She told me to pack my bag, I was being released to attend my father's funeral. Years of alcohol had shut down his liver; he was 58. I hadn't realized he was even sick.

The whole neighborhood was at the funeral, except Mom and Gerald. I'm sure Curtis didn't let my mother go, and the juvenile center didn't give Gerald up. My dad was part of the Black Patrol of North Minneapolis, a neighborhood group formed for protection against police brutality. He knew a lot of people and he was a powerful man.

But I sat in Estes Funeral Home, surrounded by people mourning his death, and didn't feel a thing. My dad was an important man on the street, but we had no father-son relationship. We never played ball or went swimming, like most kids do with their dad. I admired his status and power in the community and treasured his occasional affection when I was a kid, but I never felt secure. Like I could count on him to take care of me. So I sat there, not knowing how I should act. Was I supposed to cry or be a man? Of course, I chose to be tough. Like he'd always shown me.

A few weeks after the funeral, I was released and went back to living with my mother and Curtis. I was in my last year of high school, and I was attending classes from 2 to 5 p.m. I earned a lot of credits from the juvenile home that transferred back to my high school. I wasn't Special Ed at juvie; learning came easier for me there. I could focus better.

When I graduated in the spring, I made a decision that I would regret later: I decided not to walk across the stage to get my diploma. I knew I didn't fit in and I was afraid of being judged, I guess. Once I had accidentally overdosed in front of the school and the ambulance had come for me. People talked about it and it was embarrassing. I also didn't feel worthy. I had been put in a special class and just shoved through the system. So some of my Special Ed associates and I went and got high instead of attending graduation.

Although regrets and criticism had come down on me early, I was about to find one of God's greatest gifts for me, at a bar in South Minneapolis.

4

My Gift

When I first met Marcella, she wouldn't believe my name was Marcell. She was 19 years old and I was 17 when we were introduced by a mutual friend at The Flame, a nightclub in South Minneapolis. Two or three weeks later, when my mother confirmed my name, things started to progress.

She started out as someone to go partying with. But a couple of months later I went to her house for Thanksgiving and met her family. She had four brothers, a sister, and aunts and uncles and cousins. They had a nice home in a nice neighborhood, where there weren't a lot of black families. It was my first exposure to a real family, including a mom and dad together in the house. I was hooked.

Marcella's father worked for the city of St. Paul. He had been a bootlegger in his younger years, but when I met him, he was a Church of God in Christ reverend. While he didn't approve of my lifestyle, he was always respectful of me. The whole family treated me with kindness and respect, which continued despite what would happen in my relationship with Marcella.

I was still a senior in high school when I told Marcella that I loved her. I had never felt this way before, and it was exciting. But I was also about to fill my father's shoes more completely than I had ever wanted to.

Sexual activity was so much a part of the lifestyle I grew up watching that I probably would not have believed it had someone told me it was wrong outside of marriage; I hadn't heard that once. It was about recreation. I even let Gerald have one of my girlfriends for his first experience as a kid. But later, when I fell in love with Marcella, it became something more. My heart was now involved and I became very protective and jealous.

A few months into our relationship, Marcella and I came home late to my mother's house after going to several after-hours parties. Something sparked in me that night; maybe I felt she looked at a man the wrong way. I slapped her hard in the face. We both were shocked. I felt bad about it almost immediately and within a few minutes was apologizing.

I told her I was sorry.

I told her it wasn't going to happen again.

I told her my dad had died and I had never grieved for him.

I may have been scrambling for excuses, but I truly believed it was because I had not grieved for my father. She recognized my sincerity, and we continued to date.

But I didn't know really how to be in a relationship, except for what I'd seen. As much as I hated it, something in the back of my mind told me that violence was expected of me as a man; it was a way of showing control. In the end, it had control over me. The thing I detested taken root in me. A year later that never-again resolution eroded into regular abuse.

In 1978 Marcella and I got our first apartment together. It was in a bad neighborhood, on Broadway and Bryant. We had one small chair and a twin bed for furniture. That is about all that would fit in that apartment. Marcella was alone one evening when someone tried to break in. Terrified, she moved the refrigerator in front of the door. From then on, we came in and out of the apartment through the window. We moved out a few months later when I burglarized a furniture store, then beat my partner out of his cut. Fearing retribution, we each moved back home. That was the last time I let a partner or friend know where I lived.

Later, we moved into low-income housing on Franklin and Chicago. The building was run down, filled with people just a few steps from homelessness. One day I saw smoke coming from a neighboring apartment. I knew the guy who lived in there was a drunk. I went in, helped him out the door, and was gone by the time the fire truck and ambulance came. Maybe I see the faces of the people I love in those down-and-outers. I've always had a soft spot for them, even when I was one of them.

When he was teenager, Gerald robbed a cab with two other boys. My mother and I went to court to hear his sentencing. Because one of the boys unexpectedly pulled a knife during the robbery, the charges were upped from robbery to aggravated assault. When the judge announced that he was certifying Gerald as an adult, my mother's cries filled the courtroom. I'm sure he was in shock as he was led away to prison at 15. The next time I saw Gerald, he was an 18-year-old ex-convict.

After Gerald went to prison, I started shooting heroin and cocaine. About twice a week I'd come home high and accuse Marcella of something, or just use her to vent my emotions. After physically abusing her, like clockwork, when the sun came up, I was apologetic. I knew she wasn't telling anyone about the abuse.

Marcella lived in isolation. Because she knew I told no one our address, she never opened the door if someone knocked. She also did not answer the phone. She was home alone one evening when someone again tried picking the lock to our apartment. When I came home, I realized it was likely retribution from a drug dealer I had recently robbed. I didn't know how he could have found out my address, but we left in a hurry, with just the clothes on our backs. Marcella went back home to live, and I went back to the streets. Now it wasn't just me who felt the need to always be looking over my shoulder. Because of my lifestyle, Marcella was fearful too.

Soon we had a child, Lamar. I was proud to have a son. When Marcella worked, I would watch him, but he'd eventually end up at my mother's house. My mother weighed over 350 pounds at that time. (Her way of dealing with Curtis's abuse included sweet rolls, Pepsi, and sitting on the couch with friends watching soap operas.) By then, Mom and Curtis had two children who were old enough to help her out with things, including watching my son.

I was staying at Marcella's parents' house sporadically. A year later Marcella was due with our daughter Marissa. I had just come off of a two-day drug binge when she was going into labor and couldn't take her to the hospital. That's how I remember it. She seems to recall that I was just afraid. Someone pulled her father from his bed, and he took Marcella to the hospital. She helped me out remembering that detail, too. My children are such treasures to me, but I didn't act like it then. My days were spent conning and stealing and doing whatever else would bring in a buck.

After dropping the kids off, I would head to my usual hot spots in downtown Minneapolis. I'd scout out potential crimes or burglaries. I was also sneak thieving then: taking wallets out of purses in office buildings and taking money out of business safes during daylight hours. By this time I had a record of thieving, but I got away more than I got caught. Gerald and I worked together at times. Once I took a dolly from the basement of an office building, and we walked confidently up into the office. He pointed to equipment and checked it off a fictitious list on the clipboard, while I loaded up the goods. We must have been convincing, because the employees let us walk out the front door with their office equipment.

I took the stolen merchandise to my fences on Hennepin Avenue. The customers who bought my goods owned or managed pawn shops, a porno shop, restaurants, and a shoe-shine shop. This is where all the players went. Running the fence was my first real business. All through my twenties, I earned my living selling stolen merchandise, which included special orders they placed. The man who owned the porno shop once played a part in a sting operation to catch me. It worked, but I escaped without prison again. A local station featured all my stolen merchandise on the news that night.

I studied my profession wisely. I knew what crimes carried the most time and stayed away from those, like armed robbery. I was focusing mostly on third-degree crimes, looking for safes, cash boxes, or office equipment like typewriters (remember those? They were heavy in the '80s) and the new thing, VCRs. I would regularly walk into businesses during business hours and walk out confidently, with merchandise in hand.

There is an expression that describes me at this time: *I used to live and then I lived to use*. Have you heard it? It's about drug addiction. We start using to live, or to party and have fun, but eventually it begins to control us. Then we live for the purpose of using. Shortly after my children were born, when I was in my early twenties, I realized I couldn't function without drugs. As a result, many of my crimes were desperate attempts to maintain my habit. Like when I walked into a business, picked up the cash register, and walked out the door, assuring them that I was sent by the manager. I thank God that I am still breathing and walking around today.

My kids were often the victims of my desperation too, I'm sorry to say. More than once I took their Christmas presents back to the store to get money for drugs. Other times I went into their room and stole their money. I promised myself that I would never do it again, but the promises of an addict are nothing but good intentions. Everything bows to the habit, the addiction. Shame and despair filled me but didn't stop me.

Marcella and I were living together again, and while I was spending my days conning and thieving, she was working and collecting AFDC, what welfare was called then. My mother collected it when I was young, everybody in my neighborhood bought groceries with food stamps and lived on AFDC. I thought this was normal.

I don't remember using my money to contribute to family needs. My money was for partying. Marcella was working hard at holding our family together and keeping the abuse to herself. My mother didn't tell anyone about the abuse she was getting, either. This secrecy is a cornerstone of abusive relationships. If a woman is committed to a man, she will do whatever she can to keep it together, because she believes that she is doing the right thing. I believe personally that God has put that in a woman, the desire to stick by her man through thick and thin. It is never wrong to love someone, to want to stick in there. But it never should be at the sacrifice of personal safety.

When I drank, I was vicious, Marcella said. But she saw something in me that I couldn't see in myself. She said that I had a kind, loving heart. Of course, I felt worthless. When she would say, "I want the good guy, not the bad guy," I would tell her that there was no good guy. It was two years before she stopped believing the abuse would end. I made promises about being home and spending time with the family, then I was gone for weeks or months at a time, staying with other women. I was running. I didn't know who I was, how to love a woman, or how to be a man. The street lifestyle was the only way I knew, and even though I still felt like I always had to be on the run, it was comfortable. It was in my blood, I thought.

Once I caught a forgery charge with a crime partner, Thomas. We were both in the county jail, when over the loudspeaker we hear, "Thomas Marcell Jackson, up to the sally port." Me and Thomas and another guy all get up. I had done time with this other guy, and knew him only as Jackson. I asked him his name then, and he said, "Thomas Marcell Jackson." I had a vague memory of that name.... I told him I thought he was my brother. Later, he called home and his sister looked on his birth certificate. His father's name was Louis A. Thomas. He was my younger brother. All his life he had thought he was Native American. He grew up thinking his dad was a Native, and that he had died in the military. His father was actually a player, a man I loved, but who knew little about living in a relationship. He handed down more than I realized.

Marcella started to go back to her parents' home to get away. I'm quite sure by then her parents knew there was abuse going on. She'd go home for a week or so, until I would sweet-talk her back with variations of "Honey, I'm an addict. I want to change."

Marcella and I were together for six years before one of our separations lasted. She had finally had enough of my manipulating and lying and using her and wasn't falling for my sob stories anymore. She moved out, and I, in anger, sold all the furniture and household stuff and bought crack.

These were dark years for me. I was drunk every night, feeling like a failure because of the loss of my family, again. The few weekends a month I had with my kids were my only attempts at sobering up. I started committing armed robbery and first-degree burglary. I had no fear or respect for police officers; my crimes were subconscious suicide.

I'd been to the county jail thirty times or more. The jailers knew me, the judges knew me. Sentencing now is based on a point system: so many misdemeanors automatically become a felony. It wasn't then. Up until the mid 1980s, I was playing the same hand over and over and getting a slap on the wrist, a dismissal for lack of evidence, or short stays (ninety days max) at Hennepin County Work House.

Marcella and I had been separated for three years when I received my first prison sentence: eighteen months at Stillwater for burglary and check forgery. I was 27 years old when I went in. I would be a changed man when I came out, but not for the better.

-5-
The Big House

While I was waiting for sentencing in the county jail, a man Marcella had been dating was in my quad. After he was gone one afternoon, I found out (from my kids) that he and Marcella had gotten married. If you lived the life, you did the time. That fact was well accepted on the street. People in my neighborhood, myself included, couldn't believe that I had eluded prison for so many years. Gerald was in before he turned 18; I was pushing 30. Another fact that I could accept was that because of my lifestyle, I had lost Marcella. Later, this would prove much harder to accept than I originally thought.

My first impression walking behind those prison bars was *I finally made it to the big house.* I saw friends I hadn't seen since high school. It was like a special ed reunion. Some of my classmates had been locked up a long time. I never went out to try to hurt people when I stole, but that wasn't true for everyone on the inside. A lot of my friends were serving three, five, or ten year sentences. Some were in for life.

But I discovered perks that jail doesn't have: TV in your cell, a weight room, school. I didn't like the school part then. But facing lockdown, I went. It was here at Stillwater that I tested out at a fourth-grade reading level. If they'd had a test for confidence level, my score would have been even lower. It was part of what kept me from trying to get a normal job.

When I was in my late teens or early twenties, I had picked up applications from warehouses or for custodial positions. But with no work history and no references, even looking at the empty page was a slam to my self-esteem. Sometimes my fabrication skills, and Marcella, helped me fill in the blanks. But I often didn't have the confidence to bring the application back. When the job required you to fill it out on location, I would bring along a dummy application and just copy from it. But the idea of having a pre-employment test scared me enough to keep me away from most of those jobs.

After I had been in prison a few months, the drugs had cleared my system and I could think more clearly. I started to take a close look at my life. I was a 28-year-old addict. I had abused and lost my family. I couldn't read and write. I couldn't fill out a job application.

In the morning, I'd do my four hours of school and think about the raw hand I had been dealt when I was supposed to be getting an education. During the day, I would see people getting visits or letters and money in the mail, and I realized I had nobody. In the evening, when we would played dominoes or cards, or went to the gym to lift weights, I would hear the guys talking about wives or girlfriends, and my loneliness was all I could see. What I had thought wouldn't bother me, what I had so nobly accepted—losing Marcella—now felt like a knife in my stomach. My longtime friend and the mother of my children belonged to another man. I was betrayed. Even though I talked to my kids on the phone, I felt I had lost my family when Marcella married.

I was angry before, but after a few months on the inside, I was raging. From about six months on, my anger snowballed every day. Even hopes of finishing and getting out were doused with the realization that there was nothing to go home to. The end of that prison sentence was the most hopeless, desperate time of my life. There and then, I made the decision to get back at society for the hand I had been dealt. Someone was going to pay. When I got out, I would be slicker and smarter.

I harnessed that anger in the gym and soon was in the best shape of my life. I was lifting weights and running five miles every night before I was let out. Soon I would be free, and I would take what was mine.

When I was released in 1988 I was alone. I took a bus to downtown Stillwater and stole some beer, then hopped another bus to Minneapolis and an old friend's house. We stayed up all night and I reacquainted myself with drugs and alcohol. The next night was one that I would regret for the rest of my life.

I went to Moby Dick's on Hennepin Avenue and was drinking heavily, having a good time slamming Long Island iced teas. I got into an argument with a woman at the bar and hit her in the head with a beer bottle. I can't recall anything about the argument. My last memory is being put in a headlock by the bouncer and being thrown out of the bar.

I was unconscious, but I remember feeling like I was between two worlds, falling into a deep, dark hole. I was sinking, but I knew I had a decision: fight and live, or go into that black hole. I was tired and worn out. It was tempting to just let go and be done. But then I thought of my kids, and my decision was made: I wanted to be there for them. It took everything in me to hold on, to even breathe.

I woke up in a hospital bed, tubes and wires connecting me to life. I had lost so much blood, the hospital told my family that they did not have enough blood to give me. I also lost two days of my life.

I was highly sedated, and apparently I started cussing people out, including my mother. I remember her crying. It was her worst nightmare, any addict's mother's worst nightmare, being called to the hospital. It was one step worse to be called to the morgue. So even though I was calling my mother names in my delirium, her one relief may have been that I was laying in a bed and not a drawer.

There were things that I did after being thrown out of the bar that I will never remember. I was in an alcoholic blackout. I thought I had been shot by the girl's boyfriend from the bar. But according to the police report, after being escorted out of the bar, I had stolen a car. I was pulled over by a Minneapolis policeman when I ran a red light at Seventh and Marquette. He had me step out of the car and was giving me a pat-down when I apparently decided I needed to make a run for it. Then he apparently decided that it was a good time to discharge his firearm.

The nurse told me that I was shot near my spine, real low. The doctor had gone in from the front to retrieve the bullet, and I found staples that started at my stomach and went way down south. I had IVs, a breathing tube, a colostomy bag on my side, and no feeling in my right leg. I was heavily influenced by drugs, both the ones I carried in with me in my veins, and the stuff given for the pain, but I thought I saw Marcella in my room.

After four or five days, uniformed police officers came for me. I was put in a sick ward at the county jail, pulling my IV pole, colostomy bag nice and warm against my stomach. The truth is, I *had* stolen a car, but they could have just given me a court date with the charges pending for auto theft. Auto theft is the lowest charge in the grid, if you will. You're not considered a threat to society. But I was locked up. Because they were trying to make me look dangerous, I suppose, to justify the shooting.

In sick ward at the jail, I couldn't get up and retrieve my tray from the sally port. The other guys brought it to me, but I didn't have much of an appetite. After five days, Curtis posted bail—a couple hundred dollars—and brought me home. It may be the only time I experienced compassion from him. I stayed on their couch because I couldn't get up the steps. Although it would take me a year to walk again, I started using again on the couch. With my body broken and bruised, I continued to destroy it.

My leg had such bad nerve damage that it felt on fire constantly. Drugs and alcohol couldn't numb the pain in my leg. I ordered the doctors to cut it off. They said it would heal. That was a promise two years in coming.

A wheelchair took me the few places I could go; it would wheel right into the van that collected me for my doctor appointments and physical therapy. Helplessness added to my anger. I spent my days on that couch, cursing the fire in my leg, nursing the fire in my soul. I had nothing to show for my twenty-eight years, no home, no car, and no family. I couldn't even go out to hustle and make money. There is no workers' compensation insurance for hustlers. I was physically and financially broke and living with my mother.

Sixty days after the accident, I went to court and received probation for my auto theft. By that time I had lost a hundred pounds. I credit God for orchestrating my good physical condition before the accident; if I were in my normal physical condition, I would not have survived. Keeping physically fit was the same priority for me as it is for most addicts—which ranked about second to last, right above reading my Bible every day.

After four months, my stitches came out. When I went from a wheelchair to crutches, I hobbled back onto the street, more than ready for some action. I targeted women heavily, hustling them for their money and for a place to live.

Even though I'd had one foot through death's door and had chosen to live, I wasn't grateful for my life. I still had a hopeless attitude. I was getting a lot of DWIs and misdemeanors, stealing from drug dealers, and bingeing on alcohol and drugs for most of the two years before I caught more time at Stillwater prison. By now, I was tired and okay with it. I had started to accept that those bars were a way of life for me.

Once the drugs started to clear my system, I didn't like what I saw. My lifestyle was hurting people I loved dearly. I couldn't communicate that love to them, and my drug addiction was causing me to do what even I knew was wrong—like stealing from my kids. The shame was building, but I had tried to do right and failed so many times that I felt like I could do nothing about it. Yet as strong as that hopelessness was, it was not as strong as my hunger for success—to be recognized in the street. Maybe I could make it up to my kids—and be accepted by my family more—if I had some business going on.

I came up with a plan. I would limit my drinking to one beer a day. This was my first desire to stop drinking since I had started as a teen. The drinking and drugs went hand in hand; in order to stop one I had to stop both. I was tired of abusing myself too, and I wanted to gain some control and make it pay. I would also keep away from the crimes which would get me a felony charge. Then, in the '80s, selling drugs wouldn't get you a whole lot of time like it does now. So I planned to sell drugs to get the money for the tools I needed for the next phase of my plan: use women to support my lifestyle. I needed cars and jewels and bling to draw women in. After I had set myself up, I would ease off selling drugs, which held a bigger conviction than promoting prostitution (which wasn't considered a sex offense then).

Ultimately, I just wanted to take back control of my life. The dream of that was what drove me. I thought I had control of the wheel and was taking charge of the future. It was a lie that many fall for. I was powerless all the while.

That future I envisioned for myself included Marcella. I sat down and communicated the only way I thought she might listen, in a letter. I wanted her to understand where I was coming from, and I didn't let my horrible spelling slow me down. She was the only one who could ever read my writing, and I'm sure it was worse in that letter; I wrote like I'd never written before, whenever I had a spare minute, for two weeks.

My heart was always hers; I always felt at home with her; she made me feel whole; the other women meant nothing to me; I would come home for dinner with the kids; I loved that she didn't criticize me for my criminal or loose lifestyle, and she didn't nag me; she accepted me for who I was.

When Marcella and I were together, I knew I didn't treat her right. She was so calm and patient, and that had annoyed me. I didn't think I deserved her love. I would abuse her and push her away, but she wouldn't go. That only added to my shame and guilt. I'd never known that kind of love. She was respectful and she didn't cheat on me. During our time of separation, she would sometimes show up with dates at the same nightclubs where I was. Knowing how violent I could be, she would always do a U-turn and head back out the door. But when we were a couple, she always said that I had good in me.

I sealed my heart up in that envelope. A short time later, it came back to me with *Return to Sender* scrawled across the top. She had gotten an annulment from that other guy before he was even released, but I didn't know that until later. It was like she was finally free and didn't want to risk that freedom by responding to me. Looking back, I don't blame her. I had kept her sheltered and abused for years; I believe that she had identity issues to work out too.

At the time, though, I was hurt when she sent back the letter. Boy, did I feel like a loser. That hurt turned to anger, the emotion that prison seems to manufacture. Eventually that anger was fuel in my determination to get her back. Even if the only mail she was sending me said *Return to Sender*, I wasn't going to stop pursuing.

While in prison, I called a phone number for a lawyer off a TV commercial. The lawyer started gathering information for a lawsuit I would later file against the city of Minneapolis because of the shooting.

My second prison term ended in the early '90s, and I was sober and ready to get down to business. I was handed the opportunity at the halfway house where I was placed when I immediately hooked up with a guy who had robbed a pharmacy for drugs. I started selling for him.

In the four or five months that this work-release program lasted, I was required to have a job. I struck up a partnership with a guy who owned a computer business. He gave me a title—computer consultant—and printed check stubs for me in return for drugs. Once my case manager came in to verify my employment. Since all the other employees were in on it—I supplied both him *and* his employees with drugs—they informed my case manager that I was out on a call.

My network of customers was growing: it started in North Minneapolis and spread out from there. It required me to have wheels, so I bought a Cadillac and parked it a block away from the house, since I didn't have a driver's license.

Marcella started taking my phone calls, and I convinced her to meet me for lunch. She had never done this before. I started working on her big-time: I paid for nice meals, I told her I wasn't drinking (true, for the most part), and I gave her money for the children. I painted a picture of our future being like a family vacation. I knew *that* would throw a ring around her heart and I would be able to pull her in. At first she wouldn't tell me where she lived, but by the time I was finished at the halfway house, I had found out her address, showed up on her doorstep, and moved back into her life. We lived in an apartment on Chicago. The kids were 8 and 9 years old, and happy that I was home. I wish I had been. They needed me then, and I was in the street all the time.

This was an especially crucial time for Lamar. I should have played football with him, taken him fishing, introduced him to the outdoors. I should have been a father to him then. That I deeply regret. The consequences of my sin rooted in these years would do great damage later.

I followed the plan I had hatched in prison and used my network of customers to start selling crack cocaine. My circle of customers grew, and soon I was making more money that I ever had in my life, selling weights. My business escalated and I started gathering the tools that I needed for the next phase of my business. This is where I earned the title "Little Lou" that my neighborhood had given me as a child. I was following closely in the footsteps of a man whose street-savvy lifestyle always brings early retirement, usually in the form of a casket.

The End

I started spending three hours every week at the salon. All the pimps did it. My dad had gone to the salon to have his hair and fingernails done. He wore his nails long, shaped to a point, and painted clear. The women at the salon were paid well to make us look good, about $50 or $60 a crack. I wore my hair in long waves that reached down to my shoulders. "Fried, dyed, and laid to the side," was the saying. It was the costume of success. My plan was unfolding and I was stepping into the part.

Pimping was competition and comparison, 24/7. We compared as we talked big, and we schemed as we sat under those helmet dryers, of ways to take another man's possessions—his girls. There was a respect on the street and we were all loyal to the game: if another man took one of your women, you accepted it, respected it. There was no revenge as such. "Cop and Blow," we used to say.

Everywhere I went, I scouted for women: nightclubs, the bus station, even the mall. I would start by flattering them physically and promising them they would "make it big." I would paint a glamorous picture of the lifestyle that they could provide for themselves with me. I was wining and dining them, giving them gifts and money to help with their kids or whatever they needed. If the girl had been prostituting already, it wasn't a long process. If she hadn't been turned out yet, it took longer. It took persistence, and I had plenty of that. I was building my circle and my reputation; both were needed for success.

Once she was ready to work, I trained her, including how to please a man, then how to pick his pockets. If she wasn't willing to pickpocket one of her tricks, I would become violent with her. At this point, I had spent enough on her that I expected her to do everything she could to put money back in my pocket. Some girls had already been turned out, but it was surprising to the new ones when I flipped on them. I would slap them in the face if they didn't do what they said they were going to do—like work. This was a problem if it was cold or raining. We'd say "walk between the rain drops." I'd also hit them if they talked back, stashed money, or ran off. Most of the time they ran with my money, so I went after them. Once the girls had been around that block a time or two, they learned, and that was usually the end of it. Controlling the girls, with violence if needed, was part of building my reputation. I also protected them from other pimps, gangs, tricks, or whatever else. *You gotta do what you gotta do* was the first rule of making it.

Soon I had four women working for me. It was an around-the-clock job. I drove around every day to try and manipulate women into my circle, and then every night to take care of business. Walking the sidewalk is street hustling, the lowest part of promoting prostitution. I loved the hustle of the streets, but the best place for the girls was in the massage parlors. There were a couple in St. Paul that I used as much as I could. There were also girls that I sent out of town to dance, with a guy who made runs for us to Iowa.

When we were on the streets, I worked North Minneapolis to Broadway and South Minneapolis to Lake Street. I'd walk up and down the streets to make sure the girls were safe and doing what I had trained them to do. If the police were hot, I'd pull the girls off the corners and we'd work another angle, like the truck stops. I always had to keep my eyes open for the best way to do business, and that meant I couldn't be drunk or doped up. I had curbed my addictions in the name of business and was still managing to create an illusion of control.

I had also hooked up with someone dealing in counterfeit money. I started buying it, trading it, and using it. The FBI questioned my sister in the bank after she tried to cash in some of the money. She fingered me, and I took the heat for that. Which ended up being just a phone call. I talked to them, cussed them out even, and they did nothing. I did not even see the inside of the police station. They must have had their reasons. We got rid of the stuff after that. I had enough on my plate.

I would stay out until three or four every morning, cruising around in one of my Cadillacs. The diamond rings on my fingers flashed out the window like a sheriff flashes his badge, letting the world know who was in charge. It was a short-lived season that had to run its course. The next step was to leave God's Great Gift to me.

Marcella never tried to stop me from leaving her. And looking back, I'm not sure why I did, except pride: my lifestyle had offered me the world and I was taking it. That lifestyle, the devil, kept calling me back, even when I wanted to stay home and be a family man. I didn't know how, and besides, I was afraid to. I was driven to make something of myself.

I moved in with an 18-year-old girl who was very gullible and easy to turn out. I was with her for about three years; some of that time I was gone for four or five month stretches, doing drugs and living with other women. I had met two women in Milwaukee when I went down to visit another, and I continued seeing those two women while living with the 18-year-old. At the same time, I would occasionally darken Marcella's doorway. I didn't try to hide anything; these women all knew about one another. Then one of the women from Milwaukee had my son.

My mother had been holding marijuana for me, until people could come for a pickup. She liked the excitement and was soon selling from her house. In the early '90s, Curtis had had a stroke and was confined to his bed. She could never have done this if Curtis was himself; he would have forbidden it. But the stroke took his speech and he could only communicate through moaning. There were nurses who came to the house at first, but my mother didn't like them there when she was selling. They didn't last long. My stepfather spent the last eight months of his life alone in his room. His children, my sister and brother, didn't give him much attention. No one did. I felt bad for him. His funeral was attended by very few people.

After his death, my brothers and sisters and I would not let my mother date because she was too vulnerable. She would so easily be taken advantage of in a relationship. But she continued selling drugs. Once, I was at my mother's house with my eight-month-old son and his mother from Milwaukee. Someone came in the house with a gun and held us up while we sat at the table. I was furious and paid people on the street to find out who did it. I needed to get even.

I started to slip a little then. I had been using, but not to the point where I couldn't do business. After the robbery I started using more.

Within a couple of years, the young woman I had been living with was making trips to Iowa to dance in clubs there. I thought she was too prime for the streets. *Prime* is usually used to describe a piece of meat, I realize. It is an ugly, degrading word that judges a woman by how well she can curb a man's appetite. Although I didn't realize how degrading my lifestyle was at the time, I knew I wanted Marcella to have no part of it. I couldn't have told you the real meaning of purity if you handed me a dictionary, but I knew she was above what I was doing. I didn't want her anywhere near it. I had said to her once, "If I ever find you in a crack house, I'll beat you."

She replied, "If you ever find me in a crack house, you *need* to beat me."

Even though I had left her for the 18-year-old, I still trusted Marcella and would leave my drugs with her. And I still considered her my girl, even though I wasn't living with her. I made sure that she had everything she needed. Of course, she didn't have the father of her children, and that was what she wanted the most: to be a family. But I was still reaching out and grabbing any and everything I could, thinking someday soon that void inside me would be filled.

Through my drug dealing, I had connections that extended to the suburbs. My wealthy clients in their multimillion-dollar houses in Minnetonka gave me free reign of their homes, credit cards, and cars in exchange for the drugs I provided them. One or two of my women would stay with me; they were "dating" the men who lived there.

I had been checking on my lawsuit against the city of Minneapolis, providing whatever my lawyer needed, and it finally paid off. I was awarded $100,000, and with it I grabbed at even more of what the world offered. I moved into nice hotels with one, two, or all of my women at once. They were often driving my Cadillacs if they had to go to work and I couldn't take them. We had an understanding, and when they lived by it, life was good for them, financially speaking. I continued to expand my circle.

The two women from Milwaukee weren't the material needed for prostitution, so I faded them out and picked up two more from Chicago who had moved to Minneapolis. They belonged to a gang, and their plan was to rob some drug dealers and then head back to Chicago. They joined up with me, and when word about what they were up to made it back to Chicago, two of their gang members came up and tried to take them back. The girls didn't want to go, and I put up a fight for them. In the end, they were kidnapped and taken back. It was a huge loss for me; they were faithful hustlers, faithful employees. We had become friends. I saw one of them three or four years later. She was strung out on heroin; the other had been murdered, she said.

Gunshot was the sound track of life in my neighborhood. I was using my piece a lot. It is by God's grace I never took a life. But I was shot at quite a few times and constantly had to be on the run. I realized it was the price to pay for where I was, but it was exhausting to be living with that level of adrenaline. I was ready for change, but not sure how or what.

This was when the deception that surrounds that lifestyle started to fade; I began to realize what a lie I was living. Twenty years after my fear of being targeted in junior high, much of my dream of ruling the streets had come true. But fear was now more real than ever. I thought running the streets, being like the man I looked up to as a child, would take my fear and fill me inside. I would be The Man. But instead, I came up empty. It was like chasing an illusion. There was no reward or satisfaction.

So I went after the only source of stability I've ever experienced: God's Great Gift to me.

I bought Marcella a ring and invited her on a date. When our kids were young, Marcella had wanted to get married because of them. I told her, "I have nothing to offer you. When I do get married, it will be to you." Then, I didn't know if I was coming or going, if I would be locked up or not. I still had no security, but when I'd reached my mid-30s, I went looking for it in Marcella.

I know that if she had been the fainting type, she would have passed out cold on the floor of Red Lobster when I pulled out the ring box. There'd been no hint it was coming. After 18 years of an off-and-on relationship, we became husband and wife. During a small ceremony at her mom and dad's house, I promised to have and to hold, to love in a way that didn't require anything different in my mind. I didn't understand what commitment meant. We exchanged rings, our first matching set, which I would pawn and buy back many times over. Our daughter and son were part of the wedding party.

I was seeing two women when I married Marcella, and that continued afterward. I was still selling the dream, which included me being with them. I reassured one in particular. We had met when I was in one of my drug houses, when I was feeling the loss of the two women from Chicago. I didn't know her, but she boldly told me, "I can get you some money." She was already prostituting, and she proved to be the best hustler I ever had. She did *not* like that I had married Marcella, and she wasn't afraid to show her anger. That anger would later get her into prison for assault. At that time, I also met another woman who later became the mother of two of my daughters.

After Marcella and I married, I tried to stay home more. I found I was powerless against the draw of the street. Like when I had told Marcella I would never hit her again, the passion to stop was there, but the power was missing. Over the years, no matter how hard I tried, I always ended up doing the same bad things over and over again. It was self-fulfilling prophecy; my adult life had confirmed what I had heard as a kid. *You're no good. You won't amount to anything.* My stepdad's words replayed in my head and my former teachers echoed confirmation.

During my earliest crimes, I felt no guilt and no remorse. But by this time, my guilt, especially over how I treated my family, was so great and my shame so big, there was no living with it sober. I started using heavily again.

In June of 1994, I solicited two undercover officers in the street. They were really cool—even drove a Cadillac. I was strung out as I worked the street with the women. The undercover officers agreed to meet me at a certain motel. When I got there, they surrounded me with police cars. This was one of the things that I regret the most, because I had my daughter in the car at the time (her mother was working with me). My daughter was just a few months old, and as a result she was taken to St. Joseph's Home for Children. Their grandmother picked her up; eventually she adopted both my young daughters. Thank God for grandmothers.

Incredibly, I bailed out of that. But a few weeks later, I went down for burglary and forgery. Those charges, combined with prior charges of promoting prostitution, got me twenty-two months in Stillwater.

This time, I attended a few Bible studies. The people that I saw consistently coming in to minister piqued my curiosity. I was seeking purpose in a lot of different directions, including different religions. But nothing changed; I didn't know how to change. When I was finished with my third sentence, I packed up the plans I had made to try again, better and smarter, and I picked up where I'd left off.

Life continued in the same fog of burglary, promoting prostitution, and selling until the day everything screeched to a stop. Life changed when I helplessly watched someone hold a shotgun to my 14-year-old daughter Marissa's head.

I was sitting at my mother's dining room table with my family when three men in masks charged through the front door with shotguns. They walked out a few minutes later with our money, drugs, and jewelry, including Marcella's wedding ring.

Once again, I was furious and planned to seriously hurt the men who had done this. Again, I paid people on the street to find out. But my revenge never came. No one knew, or had any information for me. This fed that old sense of failure to protect the people I loved. It was like lighter fluid to my anger and led to yet another relapse.

There was nowhere for me to go. I knew things had to change, *I* had to change, but I also knew that I couldn't. I had failed again and again and again when I tried.

I left my house when I started using, and no one could find me. I stayed at drug houses, sometimes my mom's house, occasionally finding my way back to Marcella for a night. My frustration during this time came out strong against everybody, especially Marcella. This was one of the only times that she called the police after I was violent with her. Once again, she had to move with the kids back to her parents' house when my support money stopped. With my regular relapses, this had become almost an annual trip.

I was at the bottom and pulling my family down with me, living on the fumes of a lifestyle that I knew I had to leave behind. But it seemed part of my DNA. My strength was at zero; I came to the end of the road with no ability to hope or dream.

My last run would be with Gerald. He was released around this time, and we prowled around town like the old days, stealing a car, committing armed robbery, and selling drugs and stolen goods. Marcella's brother said that when Gerald and I were in prison, the crime rate went down. I was still running the girls; Gerald was running women on a smaller scale too. With a crack addiction that cost $500 to $600 a day, supplementing was the name of the game. Gerald and I hit several businesses in Minnetonka. When we were caught, Gerald and I went down together for the first time. The previous assault charge, along with forgery and the third-degree burglary charges, put me back in prison again.

Normally, I would play the game with the prosecutors and follow a strategy I learned long ago: fight the case, head down the road toward a trial, then end up with a plea bargain because the prosecutor didn't want the cost of going to trial. This time was different. I had a peace which started as soon as I got to the county jail. The first deal they offered me, I took. There was no fight in me, for reasons I could not explain except that I was tired of hurting people: my family, the people I was selling drugs to, everybody. I was given my longest sentence ever: thirty-three months. The sentencing didn't bother me. It was a relief not to be causing anyone pain anymore, myself included.

They generally don't sentence relatives together. So while Gerald was sent to Lino Lakes, I went back to my home-away-from-home, Stillwater. This time in, I wasn't going to be thinking about how I'd get back at society, how I'd get more money once I got out, how I'd be smarter and better in the future. I could see no future for myself.

During orientation, I was watching the ministry volunteers come in. They had peace. For the first time in my life, the condition of my heart and soul mattered more than anything. I went back to my cell and asked God why I had always felt so different from other people—why I had never been happy. I was a 34-year-old man, and the feelings I had as a teen, of not knowing who I was or where I fit in, hadn't gone away. All my life I'd had to fight and run. I was tired and I wanted peace. I went to my knees on that cold cement floor and offered the first real prayer in my life.

God, if you are real, please change my heart.
If you will give me a new heart, I will serve you.

-7-
The Beginning

I was still kneeling on the floor when the love of God filled me to overflowing. I started sobbing and couldn't stop. The Bible says God is love, and I know that God filled me with Himself as I knelt on the floor of my cell. This love was more powerful than any substance I had injected into my body. It not only filled my body, but reached into mind and my memories and covered the pain and rejection that had shaped who I was. He silenced every voice that told me I was worthless and that I didn't fit in and He filled me with joy. It was like a weight lifted off me. I stood up a man with a new heart.

I checked out a Set Free Bible from the library and brought it back to my cell. I sat and cried as I read it. Jesus said that he loved me! I knew that my mom and Marcella loved me, but this love wasn't just something I knew in my head—it filled every place in me. The Bible also said that Jesus forgave me! For the first few weeks, I confessed every sin that the Holy Spirit brought to mind. I asked forgiveness for generational sins—lust, alcoholism, drugs, sexual perversion, a victim mentality. People I never knew who carried my DNA had also carried sins that were now no longer part of who I was. I told Satan, "The buck stops here."

In my Bible reading, I came across the story of a man who was possessed by demons. Those demons drove him out to live in solitary. Jesus cast them out of the man and into a herd of pigs. Then the townfolk heard about it and rushed out to see for themselves.

When they came to Jesus, they found the man from whom the demons had gone out, sitting at Jesus' feet, dressed and in his right mind; and they were afraid. Those who had seen it told the people how the demon-possessed man had been cured. Then all the people of the region of the

44

Gerasenes asked Jesus to leave them, because they were overcome with fear. So he got into the boat and left.

The man from whom the demons had gone out begged to go with him, but Jesus sent him away, saying, "Return home and tell how much God has done for you." So the man went away and told all over town how much Jesus had done for him. (8:35–39)

I adopted that Scripture. My demons were gone, I was now in my right mind and wanted to tell everyone what Jesus had done for me.

I called Marcella and told her about my conversion. She said, "You did what?" As I explained, she was quiet. She didn't want to put me down or hurt my feelings; she also might have thought it was a new trick. When a person in prison gets saved, nobody believes the change is sincere. It usually *is* sincere, but too often offenders fall away once released because the temptation of their old lifestyle is too great. I knew my words alone would not be enough to convince her. Nor my repentance and request for forgiveness for the abuse and unfaithfulness and everything else. She said she forgave me, but I knew I would have to walk it out.

When she visited, I would bring my Bible to the visitation room to read to her and show her the exciting things I had found. She sat quietly, going along with it but not sharing my excitement. She was going to the clubs with her friends, and she didn't believe yet that things would really change for us. She'd had twenty years of me going in one direction; it would take time for her realize that I was a new man.

I'd written to Gerald a few times over the years when he was in prison, just a couple of lines with a few dollars, or a Christmas card. This time I wrote to Gerald and told him in detail how my life had been changed by Jesus and that I was now living for Him. About a week later, I received a letter from Gerald. He told me how he was tired and wanted to live for the Lord. Our letters had crossed in the mail. A couple of times in the past, Mom had told me that when Gerald was in prison, he had made a decision to follow God. This time, he had taken a big step by telling me, his brother and partner in crime.

With the timing of those letters, we knew there was a purpose for us. We would partner together for God. I wrote him back and told him that God would use what we'd been through for His glory. Gerald had earned college credits taking business classes in prison and had drawn up new business plans with every release. He wrote me back this time and said that he was putting together a business plan for a ministry to ex-offenders. We continued to pray and plan for what God might have for us.

I began school again. It seemed like I was able to focus better; I wasn't so tense inside. I was still reading my Bible every day, which was helping. But I couldn't read for very long without stumbling on a word I didn't know. I think I gave a guy two packs of cigarettes for a Bible dictionary. (Back then you could smoke in prison; cigarettes were sold at the canteen.) It was slow going – read for a few seconds, then stop to check my Bible dictionary for words I didn't understand. These were words most nine-year-old church boys would know, like *baptism*. But I kept at it. I had to know more about Jesus.

I started going to chapel whenever the doors were open. We also started a cell block Bible study. As I studied God's Word and prayed, God released me from a burden which I had carried since childhood, of feeling responsible for the physical and emotional well-being of my mother. He showed me that it wasn't my job or responsibility. For the first time in my life, that burden was lifted and I had peace. I could depend on God to take care of the ones I loved.

I read in the Bible about putting off the old man and putting on the new and I realized my whole image had to change—the way I talked, the way I walked, even the way I thought.

One of the first things that I did was cut my hair. I didn't want to identify with that old person. My hair was a woman catcher; I thought I looked cool. I wanted to ditch that image. I didn't need it at church, the only place I planned on hanging out after I was released.

During social times and meals, I had to distance myself from the in crowd because I didn't want to hear the gossip or the cursing or the talk about women. They'd tease me, "Sure you're saved in here," or "You're a Bible thumper because now you're scared, huh?" I realized I was challenging them. I was walking and talking differently, and that was intimidating to them. I took their sly jokes and slander without saying much.

Five or six months into the sentence, the Lord told me I was going to work with men just like myself, who needed the love of God. This wasn't something I embraced right away—I wanted to get out and get on with my life. But as I started mentoring and discipling men in prison, I knew I was where the Lord wanted me.

There was one man no one would talk to. He was a third-degree sex offender, a short African American guy, with one eye missing, who stayed in his cell all the time. The rejection for being a "baby-raper" is worse on the inside than it is on the outside. That conviction and reputation can get you killed. I believe that the power of Christ can free sexual offenders from that desire, just like it can free men from alcohol and drugs. I reached out to him and he started attending Bible studies. He started to come out of his cell; we started walking around the yard together, taking meals together, and lifting weights together. When I left, he told me that he'd been on the brink of suicide before we met. He recommitted his life.

I saw that I was making a difference to the men I was mentoring; I could minister and relate to these men like only someone who had experienced the same abuse, the same criminal lifestyle. I felt their pain and knew their despair.

One thing that was very endearing to me was the unity of the fellowship in the walls. But once believing offenders become believing ex-offenders, everyone goes their own way. Why couldn't we keep the same fellowship when we got out? I wrote Gerald and told him we would be opening Christian halfway homes. You know halfway homes are typically full of drugs and crime, but our homes would provide a safe place for the men to continue with the Christian fellowship and support they received in prison. When they left behind the bars that kept most of the old-life temptations out, they would have a live-in network of Christians to love them, support them, and keep them accountable. God gave me a vision for a ministry I called Christian Offenders Network Service, or CONS.

My time went fast. I served twelve of the thirty-three months sentenced, the last three or four in anxiety. Many sincere believers before me had the best intentions of following their Savior when they were released, only to fall away when they went back into their old neighborhoods. As the day came nearer, I worried constantly. *Am I going to be okay? Am I going to screw this up again?*

Baby Steps

The Lord says that when we are weak, He is strong. I leaned heavily on His strength as I took my first baby steps living for him at the halfway home. It was like the last practice before the real fight. I was scared and intimidated. I knew how to do wrong – could I learn to do right?

I wasn't associating with the guys at the house. Armed with my résumé from my job skills class, I started looking for a job. I had worked at a warehouse that delivered furniture to state and county facilities while I was on the inside. This helped me get started with decent work habits, and it gave me legitimate references for job hunting. Within the first two weeks I had a job in the shipping and receiving department of a Goodwill store in Minneapolis. It paid $5.10 an hour. I earned the first paycheck in my life working hard at Goodwill.

The first Sunday I was out, we went to the church Marcella had grown up in. They asked me to give a testimony. This was my first time speaking in public and I was nervous. But my excitement about what Jesus had done in my life overcame. It was the first time I had seen others react to my testimony; they were shouting out "Amen!" and "Halleluiah!" It felt so good to be accepted. They even clapped for me. Yet I don't think Marcella believed me, even at this point. The next week, we were invited and went out to Speak the Word Church in Golden Valley. I enjoyed the different cultures: whites, blacks, and Asians all worshipped side by side. We made that our church home.

I kept my weekly schedule and my priorities simple: work, home to my family on the weekends, church, then back to the halfway home to start the week again. Sometimes I went over to Lake Street to tell the hustlers and drug addicts what Jesus had done in my life. Once I ran into the woman from Milwaukee who had my son. She came out of a beauty shop as I was walking past. She asked what I was doing, and I told her I had been in prison and was now saved and living for Jesus. She was stunned and didn't know what to say. Neither did I. When she last saw me I was working Lake Street with my women. Now I'm passing out tracts. She was scared and I was scared. I asked about my son. She hadn't told him who his father was. I wanted to respect her decision and didn't push it.

I soon found a job that was closer to home and paid more. My pay jumped to $5.85 an hour when I started on the dish crew at Curran's Restaurant in South Minneapolis. A couple of guys from my old life would come out with their women to eat and I would go out and talk with them in my soaked tennis shoes and apron.

"You done flipped your lid, why you workin' this day job?" they said. Then they would invite me to come hang out with them.

"I've been saved and I'm living for the Lord," I said. I explained to them what the Lord was doing in my life. They listened, then cracked jokes at me.

"There is so much you could be doin'," they said. Of course, they didn't understand because they were stuck in the world. They thought I was afraid. But that wasn't the last that I would see of them.

With a regular income, I started giving away food, clothes, and money to help people. My wife said, "What is wrong with you?"

"Jesus said we got to love people," I replied.

"Yeah, but we have to be realistic about it too," she said. She claimed I believed every hard-luck story that came down the sidewalk. But I was learning the principle of giving that I keep to this day. I was learning compassion for people in need and not just thinking of myself. The more I gave, the more God gave to me. We were never without food or in want of things we needed. With the start of my job, I also started tithing.

Gerald was released a few months after me and we started getting our ministry plans rolling. I got him a dishwashing job with me, but that didn't work out for him. I started tithing from my paycheck into the nonprofit organization bank account we had

50

opened. After about two months, when I noticed who Gerald was hanging with, I told him to show me the balance on our account. It was zero. It had gone up in smoke, if you know what I mean. We agreed to part ways for the time being. His addiction was taking over and I knew he was on his way back to prison.

After six months at the halfway home I was allowed to move back home, with two more months of monitoring there. I told my kids I was sorry I wasn't around when they were growing up, to be a father to them. I told them that would change now. They believed and trusted me but had reservations, I'm sure. Lamar was 16 and Marissa 15 when we started having Bible studies morning and evening.

I had told Marcella, "When I get home, I'm gonna be like a cat; you *can't keep* me out of the house." She went from thinking it wasn't going to happen to wishing it wasn't true. I was like a drill sergeant: things had to be "in order." My home became Bible boot camp. Part of it was still my fear of falling. But whatever the reason, she told me later that she was so used to me leaving that when I wasn't leaving, she felt she had to. That was our well-established pattern of dealing with problems.

It was a confusing time for me. I was a new believer, sincerely trying to serve the Lord, and my wife had left me. I had never been the one left on the inside when the door closed. Looking back, I know it was a trick from the enemy, trying to get me to throw in the towel. *You need a drink bad,* he whispered in my ear. It was tempting.

Because of some lingering DWIs, I wasn't driving at the time. So after Marcella left, I had to take the bus to church. I was attending as much as I could at this point, afraid that I would get bored and get into trouble. I went to Bible classes, marriage classes, almost anything they offered. The world around me wasn't going to church or Bible study and so I went to the church to feel normal. I had to isolate from friends who called me "holier than thou" —but that wasn't it at all. I just didn't want to relapse. I would visit my mom when my brothers and sisters weren't around.

I took the city bus to church in my Elmer Fudd hat and rubber boots to get my dose of normal. That was humbling. But I realized something important at this point: it wasn't about me anymore. It was about being pleasing to Him. It is a process to be molded into a servant, and God was working on me, helping me to break down the need to look good and feel good in order to fit into society. My life now was about Him, and He filled me more than a lifetime of alcohol, Cadillacs, and snake-skinned shoes ever did.

In less than a week, Marcella came back to me. I had been given a mentor through Prison Fellowship, a white guy from the suburbs who was nice but didn't understand my struggles much. Yet he gave me good advice: "You were the one in prison, not her. You're the one who needs it." I had been concerned about my image and reputation for so many years, it was scary trying to find myself. I had to learn to live without a mask and walk righteously. I had to lean heavily on God's Word for each day, and I wanted my family to be doing the same thing, to come to that place of safety. But I was using the Bible to try to force my family to be like me. I knew I couldn't be demanding or controlling anymore.

The Bible tells us a man should love his wife like the Lord loves the church. He loves us as individuals, and I wanted to enjoy Marcella as a person. That proved a refreshing—and weird—journey. I had loved her since I was a teenager, yet I didn't know her as a person and didn't know how to put that love into action. I knew I had to learn how to be sensitive to her needs and wants. My desire was to love like Jesus, with no selfish motives. It was a long, imperfect process, let me tell you. It was intimidating for her as well. She was tense and angry, and eventually I came to see her frustration. I wanted the peace and joy for her that I had, yet we hadn't dealt with the root issues from the years of pain I had caused her. I had left her empty and broke and hurt for a long, long time.

We started talking through things. One day, in my frustration, I slammed my fist on the table and broke a lamp. That was an awakening to me. I realized for the first time that God had taken away my former rage. I just didn't have it. I felt silly for breaking that lamp, and Marcella knew it too. I looked at her and she just rolled her eyes. Slowly, I was learning and God was changing me. In a few months, I would learn a hard lesson about how to love my son.

I worked a full year at Curran's Restaurant without missing a day. Boy, was I proud of myself. For a full 365 days, I was in the machine technology field, operating that dishwasher. The Bible says that whatever work you are going to do, do it with all your might. I was trying to please Him in every area of my life, including work.

I started leading Bible studies at a Christian halfway house called Damascus Way in Golden Valley. The director asked me if I wanted to work for a similar Christian program in south Minneapolis called The Halfway House. I went over there, spoke to four or five guys who were on their way out of the program, and decided to take the position. I would be working as a case manager, counseling the guys. I was excited to be finally working at what God had called me to do. I looked around and noticed what other case managers wore: khakis and penny loafers. I went and bought my first pair of each.

I gave my notice at the restaurant and was given something beautiful that I'd never before experienced—vacation pay. But I took no time off. I went right to The Halfway House, only to learn that the program director had left and they were shutting down. They couldn't fill the place up and thus had no funding. The program director had been a white guy who didn't know the community or the people and didn't have a vision or the passion. This type of program was my passion, and I knew I had to do something.

"Give me a few weeks," I told them. That night, I went again to my old stomping grounds—Lake Street. I stopped and talked to one addict after another and told them about how Jesus had turned my life around. "He can do the same for you," I said.

I prayed with one man after another, and they became new creatures in Christ right there on that same dirty sidewalk where I had been running my women. Each night the group at The Halfway House grew. I had volunteers from Prison Fellowship come in and do Bible studies. Within two weeks we had twenty-five new residents, every bed was full, and I was hired on as the new Program Director.

My schedule went from 7 a.m. to 3 p.m. as dishwasher, to 24/7 as program director. Along with figuring out how to set up the programming, how to complete the paperwork for funding, and how to direct the case managers and volunteers, I was on call for any emergency that arose. I went slowly, taking one day at a time.

After getting approval through the county, I also went back to Hennepin County Work House to talk to the guys about what Jesus had done in my life. There was someone already coming in and ministering. Bless his heart, he was trying. But he wasn't an ex-convict and he didn't understand the needs of those men. When he saw the connection I had with the guys, soon I was the one standing up in front. I have been going to the Work House every other Saturday since. That was my first attempt at preaching and ministering to the inmates on a regular basis. God used this to prepare me for something I never saw coming, something He would ask of me years later. It was a good thing I couldn't see it coming.

I also volunteered to be a mentor and train mentors at Prison Fellowship. All the mentors they were sending to the prisons were white guys from the suburbs. Most of the prisoners were people of color and the mentors couldn't relate to their culture. They had good intentions, though, and I felt I could give them a dose of preventive medicine. I talked to them about not giving the guys money, about spotting a con, about being careful who you let in your house, and other basics.

There were a lot of issues that came up when I talked with the ex-offenders at The Halfway House, and I knew I needed training in how to counsel. An Assembly of God pastor recommended House of Elijah, a biblical counseling program based out of California with a satellite site in Bloomington. I applied and was accepted.

Students from all over the world studied subjects like Transformation of the Inner Man, Spiritual Adultery, and Discipling. We had classes on relating to sexual abuse victims and abusers, and how closely related the two are. We were taught how to pray with people through specific situations. I felt like my eyes were finally opened to the invisible warfare that had caused turmoil in my family. I learned that Satan is alive and well, seeking destruction wherever he can find it. But, praise God, Jesus is Victor! It was great preparation for me in counseling the guys.

One night, our instructors were talking about how having a father and a mother in the home is so healthy for the children. After we broke off into our small groups, people started sharing stories of time spent with their own fathers. I sat silently, realizing that I didn't have those memories. I had forgiven my father when I was first saved; I gave it all to God. And I really thought I was okay with this. But apparently, it was a pain that had seeped into the deepest part of me and I still hung on to it. It started to come out then in tears. Even though my dad had been gone twenty-five years, time hadn't erased the loss I felt over not spending time with him.

It wasn't lost to God, either. He knows the pain felt in those tender years can be the most damaging. A man never outgrows the need for love and affirmation from his dad. In the Bible, David said, *"For my father and my mother have forsaken me, but the LORD will take me up"* (Psalm 27:10, NASB). Again I experienced my heavenly Father's affirmation and healing. He is faithful.

He has helped me parent better with my two youngest daughters. They still lived with their grandmother, but Marcella and I were getting them every other weekend. They were preschoolers at the time, and it was the prayer of my heart to stay in their lives and be a father to them. A good father.

After six months, I graduated from the counseling program. A continued hunger and thirst for God's Word led me to a college program designed for urban workers. Classes were only two nights a week, on Northwestern University Campus. With my backpack filled with books, I felt like a school boy again. I found I hadn't outgrown the fears of inadequacy. For several weeks I regularly asked myself, *What am I doing in college?*

I still was reading the Bible at 6:30 every morning, a habit I had started in prison. Not only did that consistent reading keep me drawing near to Him, but regular reading made me better prepared for all the homework. My kids and Marcella helped me out with spelling and pronunciation. Once I figured out that I could figure it out, I wasn't afraid. I still struggled, but the fear of being incapable was lifted.

Every class was taught by someone from a different racial background. I learned about different cultures from Hmong, Native American, and African American instructors. I didn't feel like I stuck out, which is what high school was so much about. Now I was having fun. God helped me focus and gave me the strength and even the desire to learn.

After three years, a little more time than it took everyone else, my graduation day came. I went and picked up my mother so she could see her 43-year-old son finally walk across that stage and get a diploma. My family was all there. God had gently led me back to a time of great turmoil and failure in my life and given me victory. His love leads us to victory in failures we can no longer reach on our own. My mother was in tears. That was a good day.

From there I became a licensed minister, a step in my plan to become a prison chaplain someday. God's someday plans looked different from mine, I was to find out.

I was also learning how to submit to my leader. As program director at The Halfway House, I sat under an executive director who was a pastor in the suburbs. He was a paid public speaker who was getting a good salary to do fund-raising for The Halfway House.

We kind of hit it off at first because he knew I had a head for business. He was a businessman at heart, too. I soon realized that was where our similarities ended. He referred to our guys as "dumb SOBs." When we talked, if things didn't go the right way or he felt stressed, he would blow up and pound his desk. I knew he was trying to intimidate me, and I wanted to flip the desk on him. Yet I submitted. I knew that to be a good leader, I had to be a good follower. It was a learning experience, and not an easy one.

In my desire to partner with local ministries, I met Minnesota Teen Challenge Director Rick Sherber. He and my boss clashed. Trying to help me out, Rick offered me a job as a case manager. But I decided to stay at The Halfway House, where I had full control of the programming. I reminded myself that my boss situation was a season that I was passing through. I didn't know what would happen down the road, but I had to be respectful of the leaders God had established over me. I knew that ultimately God is in charge, in spite of the wrong or the right that the leader dictates.

But I still had a desire to have my own ministry housing ex-offenders. It was a big need at the time. There weren't many government agencies or churches addressing the need back then. I was always looking at homes that had potential to be halfway homes. I even had a real estate agent on the lookout for homes for me. When a house came to my attention in South Minneapolis, I told our executive director that if The Halfway House didn't buy it, I would. He made it happen. I furnished and licensed it. As required by the city, I went door to door for six blocks to inform the neighborhood about the program, promising them there would be no problem. I knew I was responsible for these men in the community.

Once, one of my guys had a drug relapse and ran outside buck naked. My house manager couldn't get him back in the house, so I got out of bed in the dead of night to drive over and help corral him in. The neighbors were already leery about us being there, and having one person freak out and jeopardize the program for everybody was one of my biggest fears.

Because I was still giving my testimony on the street and bringing in guys, the beds were usually full and the county funding was coming in. So the board wasn't checking up on our executive director, whose job was fund-raising. When we were alone, his words to me were "I'm not going to raise money for these drunks."

Once a group at a Methodist church in South Minneapolis invited us to come and speak. Other than giving my testimony in church, this was my first time speaking in public. About twenty older white women sat quietly in that basement room next to the kitchen, waiting for me to begin. It was not easy. I started with my childhood, relating my mother's abuse and hard times. It wasn't long before I noticed some of the women begin to cry. When I saw the pain on their faces, I couldn't hold my own tears back. They continued to cry as they listened to my testimony; I continued to cry as I told it. I could feel the Spirit of God moving in the room. When I was done, they all came forward and hugged me. I looked over at the side to see my Executive Director just shaking his head, a strange expression on his face. This was a good ice-breaking experience for me in public speaking. I realized that God will use my weakness, even my fears, for His glory.

While my life was taking on a greater purpose, my mother's started to unravel. She began calling me and asking for money. I knew she had met a young guy and that he was spending a lot of time with her. Now, my mother was in her sixties, didn't have a lot financially, and weighed nearly 400 pounds. She had broken her leg in the early '80s, and it had never healed right (because Curtis had taken the cast off too early), so she could barely get around without a walker. She had spent time in a nursing home and then had moved into an apartment. Because this young guy was a crackhead, I knew what he was after, and it didn't take him long. When he moved in with her to sell drugs from her place full time, I started to see one of my worst fears come true. A man reaps what he sows.

At first I didn't believe it when my brothers and sisters told me that my mother was doing drugs. Then I saw the people who were hanging around her apartment. I was afraid for her, and I would go over to her house regularly and tell her, "You shouldn't be doing this, Mom."

This continued for a time, until she responded, "This is my house, you'd better leave." I couldn't believe it. She had always been the one in my corner, and now she was putting this between us. I continued to call her until her phone was disconnected. Because all her money was going to her "boyfriend," I would give money to my brothers and sisters to take to her. The closest I could get was the curb outside, I didn't trust myself to go in; I wanted to bust in and snap out on everybody. But I knew if I tapped into that rage again, I could go back to prison.

This was the defining point of my faith. Was I going to follow my flesh and take care of business, like I had when I was living by the rules of the street? Or could I trust Jesus to take care of my mother?

Many thoughts went through my head: *My mother has always depended on me. How can I sit by helplessly? She's never needed me more than now....* But as I sat there in the dark of my car, I knew I had to trust the One who had never yet let me down. With my hands helplessly on the steering wheel, I lifted her to Jesus.

God, please intervene. Please save my mother.

Prayer kept me on the right track. I knew if I got too cocky, the devil would come in and trip me up. I knew if I wasn't careful, I could easily share a cell with any one of the men at The Halfway House someday. They were still my peers.

When I was out on the street witnessing, I would see my old crime partner Thomas. We'd talk a little once in a while, but he kept his distance, waiting to see when I would revert back to my old lifestyle. After a couple of years, I invited him to sit in my car to talk.

"Are you tired?" I asked him. He said yes.

He had been kicked out of his home state of Mississippi when he was 17, escorted to the border. By the time I met him in the late 1980s, he had found his way to Minneapolis with twenty years of drug addiction and criminal experience behind him. I took him to The Halfway House and told him that if he finished the program, I would take him home to see his mama. Soon, he accepted the Lord and was growing.

A lot of men from my neighborhood came through the program, even a couple guys I had gone to high school with. I would hang out with them at one of the other locations that The Halfway House had, watching TV and playing cards or dominoes. One night, a guy I had graduated high school with and had done time with, said, "How long you been in the program?"

"Three years," I said.

"Three *years*?" he echoed, looking at me like I was nuts. The other guys laughed and informed him that I ran the program. I was grateful to be looked on as one of them, because I was. I fit in. The only difference between us was Jesus. I knew Jesus' love could change each one of these men like it had me. And I prayed that time would not take away my dependence on Him.

At church one Sunday, I ran into one of the guys who had jigged at me when I was working Curran's Restaurant. I was excited to see him, until he told me that he was there only because a friend invited him.

"Hey man, you're really serious about it," he said solemnly. I said I was.

I knew that no matter how many years I stayed clean, it would never add up to immunity. I knew of guys who had been sober ten years and then relapsed. Anything is possible. This was made all too clear to me when I discovered crack cocaine in my basement.

I was at my house alone when I found it in my son's bedroom. The temptation was like fighting the tide; it came suddenly and almost swept me off my feet. *No one would know if I smoke it*, I thought. The attraction held me in its clutches for a brief moment. Then I went quickly to the bathroom and flushed it down. The strength of it struck fear in me and keeps me in prayer still. I am a living testimony of God's words from 2 Corinthians 12:9, *"My power is made perfect in weakness."*

I felt my weakness in more ways than one. As I waited for Lamar to return home that evening, my fear turned to rage. I was on him as soon as he came through the door.

"Don't you realize if I start using this again, it will destroy all our lives?" I yelled. I roughed him up physically and he started to cry out of confusion and hurt. Then he said something that pierced my soul.

"Dad," he said, "you've changed. I haven't."

Time seemed to freeze as the realization sunk in: he was imitating what he'd seen me do. My son learned his destructive habits from me. My anger drained out in tears for what I had done to my son. I instantly knew that I had to just love him and not judge him, because I was pushing him away.

He moved out after that. It was his way of respecting me and our home: keeping his dirt in the street. He dropped out of high school and started selling drugs full time. He lived in the madness and poison and corruption of the street that I had been delivered from. It was in his veins, so to speak, and nothing I could tell him would change him. He was addicted to the money and the lifestyle, just like I had been. He was always welcome to come back to our house, which he did most nights for dinner. He'd stay maybe a few nights a week. But he kept the temptation away from me.

Once, while riding home from work, I saw Lamar on the corner being handcuffed by the police. My son was reaping what I had sown in his life, and it broke my heart. I knew that neither words nor bail would change him now. He had to experience it and come to the end for himself. I continually took Lamar to my heavenly Father in prayer.

There was nothing else I could do for my son, but after almost a year of praying for my mother, in the car, at the curb, I decided I needed to take action. I went into the office of the apartment complex and told them I was concerned about the welfare of my mother. Then they found out which apartment was hers, they said they had been watching it, and had planned to call the Raid Unit *that day*!

You know when that Raid Unit comes in, they don't care who you are, you're going to the ground. On top of just wanting to save her from jail, I knew she wasn't in any kind of shape physically for the raid. The apartment manager agreed to my request for a delay of a couple of hours and I hustled to her apartment.

I shouted as I finally slammed open that door: "The cops are coming, you better get out of here!" One young guy recognized me on his way out and stopped and asked me to pray for him. People flooded out around us as the two of us prayed right there in the living room. Then he disappeared. I praised God for using me to help that young man call out to Him. It wouldn't have happened if I had decided to take things into my own hands.

I found my mother and got her out of the house and into my car. She was on her way to my sister's place in Red Wing before the Raid Unit got there.

Whose timing is more perfect than God's? All of our prayers and pain over wayward family members may seem lost, but God tells us differently:

You keep track of all my sorrows. You have collected all my tears in your bottle. You have recorded each one in your book. (Psalm 56:8, NLT)

I was soon to meet a woman whose tears God had collected for many years.

Thomas graduated from the program, and I rented a Lincoln Town Car to make good my promise to take him home. I found out his real name was Eugene, and I drove him down to Mississippi to meet the people who knew him as Eugene, including the woman who had given him the name.

Her name was Miss Eunice, and at first she appeared to be a tiny, frail old woman whose long gray braid weighed more than she did. But then she opened her mouth, and I realized she was a power-pack who believed in Jesus and had been praying for her son for twenty years. She hugged him tightly, and then she took my hands and thanked me profusely for bringing him back. Words couldn't describe the gratefulness she had for me. (But I knew the glory belonged to God alone.)

While we were there, Eugene took me back to the crime scene again and again while he talked about it. I just let him get it out and listened. It was his way of working through it, I think.

On Sunday, I let him drive her to church. With her eyes shining, she said, "This is my favorite day," and running her aged hands along the dash, she added, "And this is my favorite car." I was sitting in the backseat crying like a baby, so grateful that God had used me to bring them together. *This is what discipling is all about*, I thought. *Walking people home.*

While my mother was in Red Wing, she had a stroke. I found her oldest son on the Internet and called him. He said he thought his mother was dead. I told him that she was sick, and if he wanted to see her he'd better do it now. He said he'd rather keep that door shut, for himself and for his children. We conversed for a while about families and about how he felt.

I wish things had been different. When I was a teenager, the younger brother had stopped at our house. He was a white hippie and not very emotional about seeing his mother. But she cried and cried. He stayed one night, we smoked pot in my bedroom, and he left the next day. That was the first and last time I saw of him.

I would like to have known my older brothers. I know that my mother wants the same; she still holds her first sons close to her heart. She still cries.

I saw everyone who came through our door at The Halfway House as someone's family member, deserving as much respect and as many second chances as it took. I held out hope for Gerald, who was back to spending more time behind bars than not. God's Word says His mercies are new *every* morning. A man's chances are never used up, unless he closes that door himself.

One day I got a call from a detox center wanting to know if I'd take a 57-year-old white guy I'll call Sam. He came down and I started talking to him, telling him about the program and giving my testimony.

"What kind of cult is this?" he growled. He was just coming off of an alcoholic binge, and I could see he wasn't ready for talking.

"Go on upstairs and get some sleep," I said. "We'll talk in the morning."

Sam was in better shape the next day and was willing to stay. I could tell he had a business background from early on. He helped us get a lot of donations, including a van. He filled in wherever he was needed, even cooking for everybody. Our program maxed out at four months, but I managed to hang on to him for a year and a half before I had to tell him to leave. I sure didn't want to let that guy go.

Two weeks after Sam left he had a good job, a luxury apartment in Minnetonka, and a company vehicle. It looked like he was getting his feet under him. But occasionally he would come back around and I could smell alcohol on his breath.

"You gotta get some fellowship," I told him. I encouraged him to join a church or get in touch with his family. He would agree, even had contact with one of his kids. But shame had a stranglehold on him.

I like to think if he had been restored to his family, gotten into a church, or stayed a little longer with us, he would have been okay. Sadly, though, within ninety days from the start of that job, he locked himself in his apartment and drank himself to death.

I met Sam's family at the funeral. He had a beautiful wife and kids and a nice home. And a lot of friends, by the size of his funeral. I saw pictures during the slide show of a man I'd never known. He was vice president of a prestigious glass company before he fell. My heart broke for this guy who had to be forced from the fellowship before he was ready. My heart went out to his family, who were broken up thinking of him dying all alone. This kindled anew my passion to start a ministry offering long-term housing.

At this point, people were surprised at what I'd already done. One of the things that shocked people most was that I'd started a work release program with the DOC at The Halfway House. My old case manager at Stillwater prison had to come down for herself and see how an ex-offender could do it. I had been out of prison only five years at that point. I know that it wasn't of my own efforts; God was guiding and blessing.

The work release program was impressive on paper, but it made my job much more difficult. I hated turning men in but, with work-release, there is no wiggle room. If they didn't call in every hour, if they had dirty UAs, or if they didn't have a job after three weeks, we were required to terminate them from our program. If we did not strictly follow these guidelines, we could lose our license. Most of the guys came to us because it got them out of prison. I could understand that. They thought The Halfway House was an easy halfway house because we were Christians.

I tried to give every chance I could to the guys, but there were still some who would threaten me when I had to put them out. Some would go into a full-blown personal attack. One of the guys I had to terminate refused to move. After I sent a desk flying, I had to walk away to avoid further conflict. It wasn't an easy process, but I knew I had to be a professional; I had to learn to turn the other cheek. I did a lot of praying and walking away to get to that point. My old life required getting physical with whoever asked for it. My life in Christ required restraint. I can easily tell you which required me to be a stronger man. Self-control is never easy. But as always, He enables me.

The men who left would often take the keys or just break in and steal microwaves, TVs, or even meat from our freezer to sell for drugs. That required turning the other cheek and changing the locks.

People working in law enforcement usually live outside the community. Retaliation grows in a prison cell where there is plenty of time for thinking and planning. Having a work-release program was too much like law enforcement for me. I lived right there in the community, and it took me back to the old days of fearing for the safety of my family.

My heart, my passion, was in the vision that God had given Gerald and me in prison: ministry through long-term housing. I decided to step out and incorporate my ministry, Christian Restoration Services, as a nonprofit organization. I formed a five-man board of directors while still at The Halfway House. It wasn't long before we found our first house.

A few years earlier, I had been speaking at community gatherings on behalf of ex-offenders. One day we wore T-shirts with our original ministry name across the front: CONS, Christian Offenders Network Services. Minneapolis Mayor Sharon Sayles Belton was at the meeting, and she said, "Were you CONS before or after prison?" It was jokingly said, but seriously taken. Soon after that we changed our name to Christian Restoration Services (CRS).

I never tried to keep what I was doing a secret. When I told my executive director at The Halfway House about CRS, he came back with some surprising news.

"The board said that you cannot do that." He insisted that I could not be involved in another ministry. He didn't say "competing" ministry, but that was what he meant.

"Then I will resign," I told him. That was the last I heard about it from him. Yet I knew that my days at The Halfway House had come to an end.

I talked to Marcella about what I was feeling. "I think the Lord wants me to move on," I told her.

She was hesitant but supportive. "If the Lord is speaking to you, maybe we need to make this leap of faith," she said.

That was all I needed to hear. I had spent the last few years building relationships with other ministries, and I was confident I had a network, the ability, and the passion to make it happen. I met with the executive director to give my notice.

"You'll never make it on your own," he said.

"I know I'll make it," I replied. He couldn't shake me. Like the apostle Peter, I was stepping out of the boat, ready to walk in faith.

With God, All Things

Seven years after my release from prison, I was more than ready to go full time with the vision God had given me. I followed the business plan that Gerald had created while we were both still in. He was on his third prison term since we were saved.

"This is my last time," he'd tell me when we talked on the phone.

"I hope so. With God, all things are possible," I replied. I wasn't giving up on him; Christian Restoration Services and I would both be here when he came around.

It wasn't easy to get a license to qualify for funding. The county didn't want me to house prisoners in the community. But they did give me tips on how to fly under the radar; if I had five bedrooms or less, I could legally operate without a license.

The first house that CRS purchased was financed through men the board knew who paid the twenty percent down required. One of the board members put money in a CD that acted as collateral against the mortgage. The house was a five-bedroom triplex on 26th and Dupont, and it filled up quickly.

Because we had no state or county funding, I charged the guys rent at the beginning. They would arrive with just their $100 gate money, so we waited until they found a job and were paid, usually several weeks, before asking for rent. Once they did get their first paycheck, they would often relapse or leave.

We were not bringing in what we needed to pay the bills. I had full-time live-in help who worked during the week for room and board only. I was working more than full time as the counselor, maintenance guy, and chief butt-kicker, and taking no salary. That was scary in the beginning—having all the responsibility on my shoulders.

When I left The Halfway House, I had no money in the bank. Marcella was working various secretarial jobs and every penny was going to pay the mortgage and to keep the lights and gas on at home. The first year I worked thirty-two hours each weekend at Damascus Way and Teen Challenge to help pay the bills. We still weren't making it.

So I applied at Prison Fellowship for a counselor position with the men at Lino Lakes. The interview went well; I knew all the staff at Minnesota Prison Fellowship, having worked with them for years. They had pretty much given me the job, with just my reference to check before the formal offer. The only reference I could give them was my boss from The Halfway House. When they called him, he said I wasn't good enough at reading or spelling for the position. A few days later, Prison Fellowship told me they didn't think I had enough education. I didn't get the job.

Having no education gets me again, I thought. I also felt betrayed. I had given Prison Fellowship so many volunteer hours, and they knew my heart. But this I know: if I *had* gotten that job, I would never have developed my ministry. I would probably still be a case manager in prison. Those managers do a great thing, but that was not my calling. I turned my hand back to the plow and continued full time with Christian Restoration Services.

After just a few months, we had another house, also in North Minneapolis. The money again came through the help of several board members. But I knew if I wanted the ministry to survive, I needed to start fund-raising. Up to this point, I had spoken in front of groups giving my testimony just a handful of times. I felt nervous and inadequate, but I knew that God would give me the words when I needed them. As He promised Moses, *"Now go; I will help you speak and will teach you what to say"* (Exodus 4:12).

I started calling churches out of the phone book to try and arrange to meet with the pastor or outreach director. Sometimes I could get in my car and drive out to the suburban churches. I'm sure my inexperience showed, but so did my sincerity. God went before me. Some of those churches I stumbled onto would support us for years to come, like Meadow Creek Church in Andover. Another, Oak Grove in Golden Valley, let me speak from the pulpit on Sunday. Both were suburban white churches. Both welcomed me with open arms.

I started out a little intimidated when I approached an audience. In my mind, these were elegant people from the suburbs. I was an ex-offender from the projects. But I knew I hadn't authored my own mission. God had given this to me. It was His purpose for me, and I could feel His hand on my back, gently coaxing me along. That took away most of my fear. I tried to prepare, to write down my testimony, but I found sharing from my heart worked out the best.

I went ready to open my heart, not afraid that occasionally that meant tears. Like when I told the story of Sam. A few years ago, I had showed little emotion besides anger. Tears would have been a sign of weakness. Now, the thought of tears in front of an audience didn't rattle me. It was a big change that I didn't even think about at the time.

Through my speaking at men's groups, I met several great guys who were ex-offenders. They didn't want their church to know about their past, so they would call me afterward to tell me and then say what great work I was doing. My prayer was that God would put a burden and passion for ex-offenders in other people's hearts as well, so they would be open to receive them and minister to them.

That was one characteristic I was looking for when I selected men for the board. I had contacts with a lot of businessmen through my work with Prison Fellowship and The Halfway House, and I picked men with a passion similar to mine—helping ex-offenders. Since any nonprofit organization is owned by its board of directors, I knew that when I had selected the board, these were the guys I would answer to.

Although I set the board in place to keep me grounded, not to be yes-men, after a short time, my frustration with how things were running made me want to walk away from CRS. The board was busy looking at the trees when I needed them to see the forest. It was my job to set up a budget once a year; it was their job to come up with a plan of action to bring in what we needed. That wasn't happening. They were getting caught up in the details of home repair. I was willing to go without a salary to get things rolling, but they weren't looking at the future to set the wheels in motion. I had to make a decision that might cost me the ministry, and I was in turmoil about it for weeks.

Finally, at the risk of being fired, which was totally within their right, I asked them to step down. I cared for those guys, and I knew their intentions were for good, but I didn't feel like the ministry was accomplishing what it was intended for. Everyone on the board agreed to resign. I then looked for retired businessmen for the board, men I thought could give more time and get the ministry to the next level.

There was not much around for housing ex-offenders then, in part because most people with administrative skills to be executive directors didn't have the passion. And those with the passion often had no funding. Also, no one wanted to be responsible for a guy who might mess with one of the kids in the neighborhood. And although North Minneapolis was a high-need area, the likelihood of being robbed there was much greater than in any other part of the Twin Cities.

After four years and four homes and regular trips to the DOC looking for help to speed the licensing process along, it finally happened. I had shown that we could stay open and that the neighborhoods were safe. They saw I was doing some good. I'm pretty sure someone said, "Let's help this idiot out."

We were approved for a license and could stop charging rent. Our funding allowed for two-year stays, with no penalty if the men stayed longer. Still walking the streets, talking to the guys, and giving my testimony, I saw first-hand the great need for a place for these guys.

After licensing, we started getting calls to place women. We opened three women's houses in two years. With the women's housing, it takes more time, resources and money. Give the men a bowl of cereal and the phone, and they're fine. The women want two-ply toilet paper and call-waiting. Our women's director takes care of all that, praise God.

After our funding came through, I was ready to jump in with both feet and purchase as many houses as we could. While I had visions of what CRS could be, the board saw our bank account, which told them what CRS *had* to be.

I sat in on board meetings at The Halfway House, so I knew how an organization was run. Still, it was tough having my every decision approved by the board. They were all businessmen, bankers, real estate experts, and I knew their function was to help me make the right decisions. But I was the one walking the streets and seeing the need. They were all businessmen from the suburbs. I felt like they didn't understand how great the need was. This was 2001, and there were no government programs available for ex-offenders. The church hadn't tuned in yet, either. So when Marcella and I were able, I started buying up homes with my own resources and filling them with ex-offenders.

Eventually, Marcella and I turned our house over to CRS to use as a women's house and moved out to Anoka. I had originally purchased the house for an ex-offender, but he relapsed shortly after moving in. We thought it would be easier to move out to that house rather than try to rent it out because it was so far from the cities.

The neighborhood I grew up in seemed a long way from the two-acre spread in Anoka. The quiet was deafening, even scary. There was a field across the street. For the first few months, I was also a little afraid because we were the only people of color in the neighborhood. It was like a foreign country.

One day the plumbing backed up and I called the plumber. When he found out my address, he told me I didn't have city plumbing.

"You probably have to get your septic tank pumped," he said.

"My septic tank pumped?" I echoed. He filled me in on what it means to "pump my septic." Apparently, homes in rural areas have septic tanks underground that have to be pumped out every two years or so. They never told me that when I bought the house.

"You have to find a little white cap," he said.

"Where's it at?" I asked.

"Call the city, they'll have a map." The city faxed me a map, which said that it was nine feet from the front door and seven feet from the property line. I paced and measured through several feet of snow for three days. Finally, I called a guy to plow out my whole front yard. I was desperate to take a shower and get my bathroom back.

Now when I drive home, I kind of enjoy it. I would never have done this myself. But I think God arranged for me to come out here, to give me and my family a little peace and quiet.

Marcella had worked a lot of years supporting us, and it was always in my heart to bring her into the ministry, to make it a family thing. I also was still holding onto hope for Gerald. The next time he was let out, I noticed a difference in him right away. He didn't come out with a big vision or plan on how to succeed, like he always had before. And he was keeping himself—not sleeping around. He was driving a bakery truck, delivering mail, working any job just to survive. I knew that was humbling for him. He was ready to go through the lowly steps that God takes us through to build us up. He was finally humble.

"You finally got it," I said to him.

"Yeah, I'm just waiting on the Lord," he said. And I could see he was. A few months later, he married a woman from Kenya he had met at church.

The same year that Gerald started volunteering with CRS writing grants and leading Bible studies, Marcella left her almost twenty-year secretarial career to join me. She started out working half-time as the women's director and half-time as office administrator. As we began to open more women's homes, we were able to bring in a part-time women's manager and Marcella became our full-time office manager.

Now she handles the rent and the bills, gets the newsletter out, and takes care of the details that keep us floating. She is good at what she does and is well suited for it. God's Great Gift to me can even read my writing, take dictation, and spell for me. It is a huge relief for me to have her. We do clash at times. When it gets stressful and she won't do things my way, I threaten her with "I'm the boss. I'll fire you." She just rolls her eyes.

-12-
My Kin

A few months before my father died, he had gone down to visit his family in the South. I was 17 years old and at the home school when he left. I didn't even know he was going, and it was a huge disappointment that I didn't go with him. But when he came home he brought me a cousin! I was amazed to see someone from my father's family.

His sister's daughter was in her early twenties. She told me stories about family members I had never met. It helped me see a part of myself that had always been closed to me. Later, when her mom came up to visit, I finally had an auntie, too. She told me that I walked and talked like my father and that he was loose with the women. *Papa was a rollin' stone, wherever he laid his hat was his home.* I loved hearing stories about my dad.

Later, I met more cousins who came up to visit. And although I loved meeting my family, I wasn't interested in taking any trips south then. I wasn't living right, and I thought if I went down there, I would get locked up forever in some country prison.

When my life changed, so did that desire; I wanted to go and meet my relatives. I wanted to see for myself where my father grew up, his hometown, although I'd never heard him refer to anywhere as home.

So I talked to my aunt, and we decided to have a family reunion. A few months later, I drove a fifteen-passenger van packed with family down to meet the relatives I'd never known. This was way beyond my turf; the farthest south I had been at this point was Iowa.

If you ever want to really get to know your family, go on a cross-country trip with them. The road seemed to never end. Neither did the noise as I drove the Bickersons (my family would not stop bickering on the way down) to our first reunion. By the time we reached Louisiana, Marissa and Lamar were fighting so bad, I thought about leaving Lamar down there.

But it felt like I was going home. The first thing I noticed was that the people are so kind. Downtown Shreveport seemed a typical inner city, similar to where my family had lived in North Minneapolis, except smaller. You could travel a few blocks and see animals, but it was still within the city.

When I was young, my dad taught my mom how to cook hog-maws and chitlins. During that first visit, I realized why we ate them only in the winter. The chitlins have to boil all night, and it fills the kitchen with an unfriendly odor. It's hard to air out the house with 100-degree heat coming in the open window.

We had our reunion at a small country retreat. I noticed right away that we were the only light-skinned ones in the family. They didn't treat me any differently because of it. Lamar's white girlfriend was along, and no one said a thing about it.

The people I had longed for all my life—uncles and aunts and grandparents—were almost all gone. I met a few great aunts who tried to tell me about my dad, but the years had taken their hearing. I shouted with them for a few minutes and then gave up. Yet they could bake like nobody's business. They were still putting together old family recipes that my father probably sank his baby teeth into. I tasted a yellow caramel dessert that made me proud. They called it a Sock-It-To-Me cake.

I met my father's brothers through the second generation; my cousins were all in their forties. My oldest cousin gave me a picture of my grandma from the early 1900s. I could see my dad in her face. It gave me a feeling I had not had before, of being a part of something or somebody.

There were about sixty people there. It made me smile to see how much family I had. I found out that I came from a family of addicts and alcoholics. Everybody drank. But I loved them. I went around the corner of the building and cried in gratitude to the Lord for the chance to meet my father's people, my relatives. The Bible talks about Him giving you the desires of your heart, and that was exactly what it was. We had plenty of food and fun and it was beautiful.

Years before, some of my cousins had been up to Minneapolis and had seen me in action with my big cars and women. But now I was saved and sharing the Gospel. I wasn't talking the slang or drinking the beer with them. I think that put a barrier between us. Still, everyone was kind and respectful. The kids, too. They said "Yes ma'am" and "Yes sir" when they spoke to adults. I saw them get popped real quick, by more than just their parents, for being disrespectful. The kids are still bad, like anywhere, but they're respectful.

On Sunday, Marcella and I went to a Baptist church and saw a lot of black men being the head of their house and bringing their families to church. It made me proud. They may have been raising hell on Saturday night, but they were in church on Sunday with the family. It was beautiful. I don't see that too much in Minneapolis.

Much of the food we had down there I'd had growing up, like mustard and collard greens. But their recipes reached back much farther, and the food tasted better. Hog's head cheese seemed to be part of the culture too. I saw a lot of folks go into those one-stop Charlie convenience stores for a beer and hog's head cheese and crackers.

One day, my aunt's husband, Uncle Wallace, said, "I'll show you something, boy." He took me to a farm by a dammed-up river. A couple of white hillbillies put down a net and pulled up a catfish. We threw him into a metal tub and took him to a slaughterhouse right there by the river. Inside, some old guys cracked those fish on the head with a metal pipe. They weren't playing, and it shook me up a little. *Should I run now or should I wait?* I thought. But they used those pipes only on the fish, and we took the catfish home and cooked it outside. It was delicious. My wife couldn't get enough of it.

Uncle Wallace also took us to his brother's house in Arkansas. There we met his family and ate raccoon. All the old guys were saying, "Give me a piece of that coon." They fought over it. I tried a little piece of it, but it tasted too wild for me. Someone ate the piece I left. They probably thought, *Who is this northern punk?* But we had a great time. That was the first real farm I'd been to. My daughters were about 9 and 10, but didn't go back to see the animals. They were probably a little afraid.

Since that first summer in Shreveport, we've gone every other year. Each time, we also swing by Columbus, Mississippi, to check in on Miss Eunice for the day. She calls me her son. And then we drive over to Biloxi to see my sister Lisa. She was the one I used to see around the projects growing up. It was awkward then. Now she is a believer, and we have a wonderful time of fellowship in the Lord.

When I was growing up, I stayed close to North Minneapolis and saw only life on the streets. The Lord has now allowed me to travel. It has been a blessing to be able to see a little of the world with all four of my kids. It has broadened their thinking. God is so good.

I love the South. I love knowing my family. Marcella loves knowing she can have catfish every day. Each trip down, I see lives that have been torn apart being put back together and families made whole again. And each trip, I get to know my family a little better. Praise God, He is the mighty Restorer.

-13-
Church

For six years, my family and I went to Speak the Word Church in Golden Valley. It was a nondenominational church with a great multicultural atmosphere and wonderful teaching. But after a while, I wanted to become more a part of the North Minneapolis community, so I started looking for a church down there.

What I saw in most inner-city black churches was the pastor and his wife sitting up front and getting all the recognition and the glory. I didn't feel comfortable worshipping in a church like that. I wanted the church to glorify Jesus only. I looked for a year without feeling the call to join any church. I was leery about being tied down to one denomination, too.

I was also looking for a church that would let me rent space for a Bible study for the men. I went and talked to a pastor at a Methodist church in North Minneapolis, and he offered me the keys! This pastor didn't know me from Adam. I didn't want the responsibility of having the keys, but I took them eventually.

While my church search continued, one of my guys living in the house on Dupont, who was a musician on the worship team at another church, asked a question that would pull me miles out of my comfort zone.

"Why don't you start a church?" he said.

"You find a preacher and I'll support him," I said.

"You do it," he returned.

I'm not sure how I answered, but I'm sure it was some version of "Not happenin'." However, I agreed to pray about it.

To me, pastoring means shepherding people, but also studying and preaching. I loved the first part. I was shepherding the men at my houses constantly. But studying and preaching were not my gifts. I couldn't read or study well. I definitely didn't want to read in front of people. I didn't want that much opportunity to make a fool of myself or dishonor the name of God. It's different with the guys at the Work House, because they're guys. I could just level and be blunt with them. I wasn't sure I could communicate with other people.

But I prayed. *Thank you, Lord, for giving me the gifts you've given me, which You know don't include studying and preaching and teaching. You don't want me to become a pastor...right?*

I continued without a thunderbolt from God, but eventually I came away with this impression: *I'd rather have tried and failed than never to have tried at all and regret it.* God promised that He would give me the words to say (Exodus 4:12).

We formed a core group for the church and hammered out our primary objective: to provide a safe place where people would feel loved. So many of the inner-city churches tend to be "holiness" churches, where unconditional love is not practiced. How could an unbeliever see God without it? People should be loved, regardless of what they've done. We wanted our church to be accepting and loving.

Before the church opened, I went to Florida with a friend from the core group to check out a Christian aftercare ministry. A huge fence surrounded the entire complex, and trailers where the men lived were scattered throughout the acreage. They seemed like cattle, all fenced in, and it burdened me. I started to think of the two or three thousand men I had worked with over the years. I could count on one hand how many had gotten it—who were surrendered, back with their families, and really prospering in the Lord.

Later, as my friend and I stood looking out over the ocean, I asked the Lord why the success rate was so low with these men. In His still, quiet voice, He told me, *People don't make me Master of their lives. I have to be Number One.*

Out loud I said, "Church of the Master."

"Church of the Master's Love," my friend said. And so it was.

Someone from another church helped me to get the bylaws down. They gave me their old paperwork, and we reworked it to fit us.

We started out with about ten people. The guys from the houses were welcome to attend, but not required. It was within walking distance for them.

After a few years, Church of the Master's Love rented our own building space. It was the lower level of an old building downtown, and it was a dump. We started with $200 in the bank and rehabbed it by faith: gutting it and putting in a new furnace, a bathroom, and a classroom. It took me and ten of the guys from our houses three months. Our storefront church now sits in my old neighborhood on Lowry Avenue in North Minneapolis. During the grand opening, the men testified to the similarities between the rehabbed building and their own lives. It was therapeutic for them, bringing something useless to great purpose. It was a hands-on object lesson as we worked, right down to the crooked altar. We didn't want it perfect: it was symbolic of imperfect people doing work for a perfect God.

It brings me great joy when an ex-offender can get his family back. I'm happy to say we are getting more families at church: men bringing their families or getting married. Glory to God, we now need more than one bathroom! Our building will be sold soon, and we will likely rent a bigger church building in North Minneapolis.

Our mission statement reads: To provide a safe place to be restored by the power of Jesus Christ. Many of our members are ex-offenders who have left or been asked to leave other churches. We have a white ex-offender from Apple Valley who was recently asked to leave his church once his past fraud conviction became public knowledge. We're glad to have him.

It has been a joy to watch the small miracles take place in that small storefront church. We are a church to the unchurched; they aren't surprised then we don't stick to a schedule every week. We try to let the Holy Spirit lead, sometimes spending the whole service worshipping and praying over people.

The Lord has blessed us with a great ministry team. Our initial worship leader was a Hennepin County investigator. We now have a DOC officer on board. People formerly on opposite "sides" are coming together to worship the Lord and serve the people.

And that is our goal: to serve. Twice a month I open the pulpit to the associate pastors, who include Gerald. You should hear that boy preach. He's good. For me, it is a long walk of faith from my car to the pulpit. It never gets any shorter. But it keeps me on my knees.

-14-
Marcella Speaks

When Marcell was in prison for the fourth time, I was ready to walk away from our relationship for good. I kept rehearsing versions of "You can do whatever with whoever, I am *so* done." We'd been together, off and on, for 18 years, and it had been a long time since he had shown affection that wasn't manipulative. But it wasn't always like that.

When we were still teenagers, he took off his green cashmere sweater and slipped it around my shoulders when I was cold. That was the man I fell in love with. We had fun together, going to family picnics and to Valley Fair. He never could see the good that I saw in him. To me it was obvious. Marcell would offer to run to the store for my mother and refuse to take her money. He would do this even when we were separated. He treated my parents with kindness and respect. He treated me the same way, until three months into our relationship.

I was caught off guard when he slapped me. He told me with tears in his eyes that he would never do it again. He did it because he had never grieved for his father, he said. I had never lost a parent, what did I know about that grieving process? So, because I had already started to fall in love with him, I chose to forgive him. I believed him the first three times it happened. Each time I thought it was all over.

It was just the beginning. We started living together and things intensified. If there was anything out of order, if there was a piece of paper on the floor and he was angry, I got hit.

We would still go to the bars together, but he started bringing me home and going out by himself. After he took me home, his staying out became later and later until he was gone for days at a time. I knew he was seeing other women, but if it kept him from hitting me, I could overlook it for a time. I know that sounds strange. Things started to look up once I got a job and took a class. As possessive as he grew to be, Marcell never stood in the way of me working or going to school.

It took a lot of courage to leave. I had to look over my shoulder wherever I went. He would hit me the first chance he got and tell me I had to be with him and only him. Then he would buy me gifts and tell me he loved me. (I know he meant it when he said he loved me, but he did not understand love or how to express it.) I always had to hurry and get where I needed to go and then get home; he seemed to show up wherever I was. It was so exhausting to me, and I hated him so much for it, that I contacted a guy I knew to buy a gun. We arranged to meet for the purchase. While I waited, I thought about what would happen when I used the gun on Marcell. I felt like he had already locked me up; there was no way I wanted to do real jail time because of him. I also knew a little about the miserable life his mother had lived. With Marcell gone, she would be in that much more pain.

I didn't buy the gun.

As time went on, he stayed away more and I realized something: I missed him. I wanted him around again. I know that sounds strange too. Yet it was the pattern of my life with Marcell: I would pray and beg God to take Marcell away, then pray and ask God to bring him back.

Once we had children, I saw that Marcell was a good father. He loved and cared for our son, and then our daughter. I tried to ignore the other women, and I did what I could to lessen the abuse, like keeping the house immaculate. Now, before he would leave for days, he would make sure things were taken care of at home. It made sense then. But now I realize that home was never taken care of because he was not there.

When our children were first born the abuse subsided. But after a few years, it came back just as bad or worse when he drank. It had gotten a little easier to leave him and I did what I had to do to survive with the kids.

As the years passed, I grew more and more tired of him treating me the way he did: the other women, the jail time, and the drugs and the alcohol that made everything worse. The *I'm sorry*s were not working anymore. My desire to be with him, to be a family, no longer overshadowed everything else. I guess I grew up and did not want this kind of life anymore for myself or for my children, and I left again.

Life continued for me as a single mom. I hated him so much then and wanted to be so rid of him, but I couldn't be. I couldn't even say my name without saying his first. He had taken so much of my life. If a guy I met had any of Marcell's characteristics, I stayed away. If he had a birthday the same month as Marcell's, I was gone. The two children I had by Marcell were reminders enough of him. At that point, it was no problem to fend off the charm that he so easily cast out to try and reel me back.

In February of 1993, Marcell had started reading and studying the Bible. I know he doesn't remember this, but he did. He and my father talked about the Bible. And Marcell would read it on his own. I noticed a change in him right away. His mannerisms changed; he was not as rough. I thought, *Wow, maybe he has really changed this time.* When he shocked me with a marriage proposal, we hadn't really even been dating. After my initial comment of "Why would I want to be cursed with you the rest of my life?" I said yes. He had even spoken with my parents and asked for my hand before asking me. We set the date for Thanksgiving time. I continually asked him, "Are you sure you want to get married?" He assured me he did. He had always said that if he ever got married, it would be to me. Yet the proposal seemed to come from nowhere.

After his next prison term, the interest in God was gone. He was not reading his Bible anymore, and the old Marcell was back in full swing. We didn't talk or plan much for the wedding. Part of that couldn't be helped. In June, my father was diagnosed with cancer; by October he was gone. Marcell's stepfather also died that year. And then, after a third sudden death in the family, Thanksgiving came and went with no wedding. Marcell was also doing drugs again, and ended up in jail.

But, like usual, he started to pursue me again once he was on the inside. We set another date. He was released, but ended up back in jail the day before we were to get married. I thought, *I'm not supposed to get married to him.* Yet he called and told me to come bail him out so we could get married. I did. On the way to the car at the jail, I said, "If you didn't want to marry me, you could have just told me." We laughed, went home, and the next day we were married.

It seems to me that things started out better. He told me he wasn't using anymore and I could tell he was really trying to do good. But the temptation was driving him crazy and pretty soon he started getting high. That led to his fourth prison term and, a few months later, to the day I was ready to tell him we were through.

I went over it in my mind, trying to gather the courage that I needed. He called when I was in the shower, and when I got to the phone, ready to give him the ax, he beat me to the punch.

"I can't keep treating you like this," he said. "I will give you a divorce." It knocked the words out of me. Who was this man?

"No," I said slowly. Even as it left my mouth, I was looking around the room for who could possibly be saying it. I couldn't believe I was hearing myself back down. My resolve had vanished with his change of heart.

It was shortly after that when he called me to tell me he was saved. I had my doubts. He had told me so many times over the years that he had changed. It was one of his "come back to me" lines. But the tone in his voice was different. And the next few days showed the change as I spoke to him over the phone.

I had my good guy again. I had the guy I had fallen in love with, before drugs, before alcohol, before the other women, even before our kids. I had the man who made me laugh, who took me to the show, out to dinner, the guy who made me love him. He was now sensitive, compassionate, caring, loving. I knew he had been there all along. But I didn't know how long he would stay.

I was looking forward to being a family again, and the kids were happy, too. But I still had doubts. I enjoyed the change, but couldn't let myself get my hopes up about it being permanent.

After he came home from prison, he changed yet again. Everything had to be done in order, and there was no disagreeing. It was a side of him I don't think even *he* knew existed. Talking to him did not help, so, like usual, I left. He still had care and compassion, which became so much a part of his life after he was saved, I just didn't see it flowing in my home.

It was scary for me: I thought that I would have to live with a drill sergeant for the rest of my life. But I realized I was running from my problems. We hadn't invested so much time in our family for nothing. I was gone for one week, and when I returned, I found the man I loved was back. Our home was our home and no longer a boot camp.

We've traveled a long road since then. But one thing has not changed: Marcell. It took me seven or eight months to really let myself believe the change was permanent. At the beginning, I thought, "He's home. He's here. He's sober. What's going to happen?" I saw the craving to use come back, and it was strong. I think he thought he was doomed to live his life as an alcoholic and drug addict. There was no sobriety in the family. But I was so impressed with how he locked in and found another way to deal with it. He didn't feed into it.

I always knew that there was a God. I knew He existed and answered prayers. I just didn't know the full impact He could have on a person's life until He changed my husband. For a long time, it surprised me when we had a conversation and Marcell actually listened to me. There was a time when I couldn't even imagine him submitting to anyone or anything. Now, he apologizes to me, with sincerity. There is nothing that can make that kind of change, except God. Marcell is truly a new creation.

For the first few years after Jesus changed me, my biggest fear was that I would run into an old friend or girlfriend and blow it. I had seen many ex-offenders follow Jesus and then turn back to their old lifestyle because of peer pressure, or because they were ashamed after making a mistake. I knew that God would forgive me my mistakes, but I was fearful of taking even one step in that direction. So I kept a Bible in my pocket, and when I felt weak or tempted, I pulled it out and read.

The Bible says, *"Let this mind be in you, which was also in Christ Jesus"* (Philippians 2:5, KJV). That was a continual challenge. God is not a setting on your microwave—two minutes and poof, you're done and just like Him. It is a long process to learn to be like Him and be able to trust Him with your life. The tempting thoughts still came into my mind; that was something I couldn't stop. No one can. I had to rebuke the devil a million times some days. It was such a foreign lifestyle for me, that I continued to draw near to God for help and protection—starting first thing in the morning, as I had started in prison, and then throughout the day with my sword of the Spirit close at hand (Ephesians 6:17).

Three years after my new life started, I was sitting in church when I heard the Spirit of the Lord say to me, *Now it's up to you.* For one terrible second I thought it meant He had left me. Then I remembered the Bible verse that promised He would never leave us (Hebrews 13:5; Deuteronomy 31:6). Instantly after that, I knew the Holy Spirit was saying to me that it was now up to me to make a conscious decision to do right.

During my honeymoon time, right after I became a new creation, God had an extra hedge of protection around me. I believe that God has protection for all believers, but I know that during those first few years, I had an extra dose. As I abandoned everything I had ever known and threw myself down before Him,

He was diverting people and situations from my path until I could get my spiritual legs under me.

Once I understood what the Spirit was saying to me that morning, I was afraid. I had noticed that everything I touched was turning to gold, turning into a blessing. I knew it was because of Him. I felt a closeness to Him that I was desperate not to lose.

It wasn't lost. He still walks with me and talks with me and tells me that I am His own, as the song says. There are times when I feel not as close to Him, but I know that His Word is the truth, not what I feel. He promised to stay with me. When I make Him my first priority of the day, His strength keeps me. If I remember that it's about His strength, not mine, I'll be okay. More than okay.

God has blessed me beyond what I could have seen. CRS has been averaging one house per year. We have three apartment buildings—two for men and one for women. The city of St. Paul is giving me a thirty-year grant on a building for homeless women offenders. Also in 2009, CRS was awarded $1.4 million in federal programming money earmarked for homelessness, which we used to purchase and rehab an apartment building in North Minneapolis for homeless ex-offenders. The Hennepin County commissioner and a city council member spoke at the dedication ceremony and thanked me for the work I've done in the community. That was a first. Not so long ago, I was a liability. The leaders of the community wanted me locked away for good. Now I'm an asset, glory be to God. The apartments all rented out before its dedication.

My plan has always been to serve, and God has blessed me in it. The Bible says he who is faithful in little is faithful in much (Matthew 25:23; Luke 19:17). God has blessed me with more as I've shown him my faithfulness with little. I knew that I would succeed if I was obedient and using those resources, like the homes, to help people. Now that I have learned a little about real estate, I've been able to acquire houses on my own to rent to ex-offenders.

God has blessed me with material things, and it's nice. But acquiring things is not what life is about. When I was in the world, I had material things. What means the most to me is that I can be an example for Christ and a role model to my wife, my kids, my ministry, and my brothers and sisters. That is the most important thing I am doing. One of the kids I grew up with, our "cousin," said, "When God touched Marcell, he touched us all." When he saw me, he saw God in the flesh, he said. They knew better than anyone what I was and what I had come from.

God has given me strengths that Satan had a hold of in the beginning, like my entrepreneur spirit. You can believe that God's great plan did not include me selling stolen cigarettes on card tables to women on welfare in the projects. God has brought me back to His plan of goodness. He has given me something I am passionate about: managing my houses and shepherding people from the street. I do it with a heart given to me from God, the One who created me and calls me His son.

But I could not work in aftercare if it weren't an assignment from God. You get used up and spit on regularly. In a halfway home, the average stay for a Christian counselor is two years. My heart has always sided with the down-and-outers, but to be able to love and support people who continually fail is something that isn't in me. Over time, God has taught me how.

I often meet people who are in it for reasons other than to love and serve. That has been my biggest struggle. I run up against a lot of arrogant and controlling volunteers and "leaders." I have had volunteers who come in and then steer the most responsible men into their own ministry homes; volunteers who take things donated to CRS to their own ministry; a volunteer who arranged to meet with the board without me there, with a promise of "taking things to the next level" if he were in charge instead of me. So many times, volunteers come in only to vanish after they find out where we get funding. Later I see them trying to start their own ministry. But people and ministries that aren't in it to serve do not succeed in the long run.

Recently, CRS came up with a long-range goal of having 1,000 beds in five years. That's 250 beds a year. It seems aggressive to me, but I have seen and experienced God's work and know nothing is impossible. I will get behind wherever He takes us.

Where do you want God to take you? He can turn your life around. Even if you have tried a million times and failed, now is the time to start again. Don't let shame and condemnation keep you from turning or returning to God. He knows what we're going to do before we do it; our sins don't surprise Him. Hear a word from Gerald:

Many years ago I remember calling home from prison and telling everybody that I had met Jesus and had been saved. Well, that lasted for a short time after I was let out and soon I was back into the same old things.

After six more months of criminal activity, I was in prison again, and I turned back to the Lord. Once more, I had a new lease on life and was ready to serve Jesus. Marcell and I had this great vision to build a ministry that would help people coming out of prison. He had a job washing dishes and I joined him in the dish room. That lasted a few months for me. I had a plan to build this ministry and I knew it was a mandate from God Himself, so I left the dishes and began to build the ministry.

I went door to door trying to drum up support for the cause. I knew that this was the right idea, and I was trying with all my might to make it work. But eventually I got discouraged, and began to look back to the old way of doing things. Here I started the slide of destruction. Leaning on my own understanding, I began to question God and this new way of living. How come the doors aren't opening fast enough? *I had the plan and I had the ability, but I didn't have the most important part: patience to wait on God. So again I turned to the world for answers and I received what the world had always given me. I would return to prison three more times before I got Jesus out of my head and into my heart. When I finally figured out that I couldn't figure it out, things started to turn around for me. I realized that there are no plans of my own that can help. It is always and only about Jesus.*

Our plans don't turn out like we expect, do they? But His good plan for us does not change, no matter how many times we've messed up. "'For I know the plans I have for you,' declares the

LORD, 'plans to prosper you and not to harm you, plans to give you hope and a future'" *(Jeremiah 29:11).*

God has a calling for you, and it is to become part of His family. Don't let the lie about family heritage buy you out. I am no longer just the son of a pimp and his prostitute; my Father is the King. I am greatly loved and part of a royal priesthood. Won't you start again today with Jesus, and join the family?

Please contact me if I can help in any way.
Rev. Marcell Garretson
Christian Restoration Services
7957 Commerce Circle
Fridley, MN 55432
763-566-2888 (office)
612-749-0227 (cell)
crservices.org